Pleasure, Pain & Passion

SOME PERSPECTIVES
ON SEXUALITY AND SPIRITUALITY

JIM COTTER

EXETER

❖❖❖❖❖❖❖❖❖❖❖❖❖❖❖❖❖❖❖❖❖❖❖❖

CAIRNS PUBLICATIONS

1988

© Copyright by Jim Cotter 1988
ISBN 1 870652 02 9

First published April 1988

Further copies of this book are obtainable from

Cairns Publications
47 Firth Park Avenue, Sheffield, S5 6HF

Printed by The Devonshire Press Ltd
Printing House, Barton Road
Torquay, Devon, TQ2 7NX

CONTENTS

Preface

MATTERS of sexuality and spirituality affect us all. Indeed, the sexual and the spiritual impulses may be the most significant, if not the most immediately powerful, in our lives. But they are not easy to understand, nor are they easy to live with creatively. As a priest and counsellor, I have been privileged to listen to the often painful stories of those with whom I have journeyed for a while. The gift of their trust has meant much to me, and has taught me more than I can say. Their stories have echoes in my own: indeed, they have often challenged me to a deeper exploration of what is problematic for me personally. Doubtless something of my own story is discernible between the lines of these pages.

I write for those who share in the human quest for meaning and purpose in life and who have begun to focus that search on love – whether they spell that word with a small or capital letter. This book is certainly no finished product. Its second subtitle might well be *Work in progress*. Its aim is to invite further exploration and conversation. We need to continue to listen to one another as we discover more of ourselves as sexual human beings, loved in God and challenged to incarnate that love in our bodily lives.

The book has emerged from lectures given at the invitation of the Clinical Theology Association during their annual conference in 1986. I am grateful for that opportunity to think on these things and to the members of the conference for their stimulating response.

Publishing one's own work, especially on issues of current debate, does allow the time lag between manuscript and reader to be much shorter than is usually the case, but one more readily falls prey to deceits of heart and mind. Whilst final responsibility is undoubtedly mine, I am all the more grateful to Father Bernard Lynch, Canon Eric James, and

Sister Lavinia Byrne for their helpful comments, as well as to Mr Alan Dodson, typographer, for his cover design and for his critical and kindly eye, and to Mr Peter Gay of the Devonshire Press for easing the book into print.

JIM COTTER, *January* 1988

I
Introduction

THE rash and the headstrong may commit themselves to paper without pause. Most of us mooch around in an anxious state, doing anything but take up a pencil and begin – not least on this theme of two very mysterious powers in our lives, the 'sexual' and the 'spiritual'. (I put the two words in inverted commas for now because their definitions are by no means obvious.) We may read about these powers, yes; think about them, yes; converse about them, yes, more than men and women used to do. We may know what it is to strive with them in our living, but to write about them with that dubious authority of print that seems to take away the last remnants of uncertainty from the author's scribble?

To write about sexuality is foolish enough, to write about spirituality equally so: there is mystery here, and energy, and confusion, and vulnerability. It is difficult to write clearly about either; to see how they might be *connected* seems impossible. But I am compelled to try because it is so exhausting and destructive keeping them apart. My culture and my religion hardly help. Their history has left many conflicts unresolved, conflicts that are all too apparent in the lives of those who come with their stories to counsellors and priests. I have been moved by their courage as they have striven to arrive at that inner place where they can receive the gift of a greater wholeness than they have so far known. And where there is no final resolution there can be an increased awareness of how to use the conflict creatively, not least because it is seen in a new and wider perspective.

We tread on uncertain ground. We often feel uneasy in our day to day relationships. Jokes about religion and about sex can explode in the teller's face: they soon verge on the blasphemous and the obscene. Most of us would agree that there are such categories, but few would agree on where to

I

draw the lines, and the attempted definitions in law have never been satisfactory. We continue to be ill at ease, and it is often that sense of faint disturbance that first leads us to go deeper into these matters in our own lives.

Unresolved questions touching vulnerable places and affecting us to the roots and fronds of our being, and no two people coming up with exactly the same answers – no wonder it is rare for us to be relaxed and warm, not surprising that humour soon degenerates into the uneasy snigger or the strained shriek.

Mind you, the joke may be on us. We may be fooling ourselves by taking sex and God too solemnly, imagining each to be threatening and overwhelmingly powerful. Fear easily exaggerates a power that seems to be over against us and may be hostile towards us. Perhaps our perspective is faulty. We may be looking as it were into the distorting mirrors of the funfairs of our childhood. Some demystifying is in order (which is not the same as removing the deep sense of mystery). Sex is not an unmentionable cosmic explosion – even across a crowded room. God is not a despotic monarch before whom we cringe and plead on bended and petitioning knee. Both can show us the human face of love: we can learn so much about love by *being with the other* – the human partner, friend, spouse, beloved, and with the human, decisively and totally human, and decisively and totally other, Jesus of Nazareth.

That could be good news to the poor, whose authority in these matters can be trusted more than that of the powerful. For the powerful try to convince us that they have the answers, and try to impose those answers in the name of order – or is it wealth, property, the status quo? To be poor is to be stuck, to be unable to move, to be oppressed, hard-pressed by any power with which you have no relationship, in a position where you have no influence over events. Sex can be that kind of power. 'The authorities' sometimes exercise power in that way. Too much Christian teaching has implied that God is like that, especially in his less congenial moods. We need to listen to the

God who identifies with the poor and outcast, we need to listen to the voice that comes from the neglected parts of ourselves and is usually drowned by the surface noise. The issues are serious and wide-ranging and complex. No one contributor to the exploration dare write from some Olympian height of calm and resolution. The German poet Rilke knew the contrast between the tumults of his personal life and the calmer waters of his prose. He wrote a series of letters to another, younger poet which are full of insight and wisdom. But in the last of these he is at pains to correct any impression that his life was as untroubled as his words might seem to imply. Indeed he thinks his correspondent's life is far in advance of his own, but that the various griefs and hardships which he had endured had helped him to find the words that seemed to be of encouragement to others.

I don't know if my words will be simple or quiet or comforting. They may be complex, noisy, and disturbing. But I shall strive at least for clarity, even if it is only the *first* clarity. Let me explain. Von Hügel advised any speaker to lay her prepared material on one side and to await the second clarity before revising it and giving her talk. This deeper clarity would arise out of struggle and silence and a continuing to look into, to contemplate, the matters of her concern. Then she would speak in truth and with quiet conviction. On issues of sexuality and spirituality today, no writer can hope for more than the first clarity.

Further, the process from first to second clarity is only in part an individual one. At the conference of the Clinical Theology Association, mentioned in the Preface, the content of the earlier sessions was fed by a number of moving letters that had been sent to me beforehand by participants, and some of the later sessions were influenced by the contributions of others at the conference itself. I am indebted to them all. The exploration is indeed a corporate one. Without that contribution of other people these words of mine would at best be mildly eccentric and at worst dangerously misleading. However, explorers beyond the frontiers inevitably have to take some risks and they will necessarily invite scrutiny of what they report.

2

Gathering metaphors

JAMES NELSON makes a high claim for sexuality when he describes it as the central clue to what God is up to in the world. But clues are not obvious: they rarely yield their meaning at a glance. Sexuality is full of ambiguity and subtlety. It may even be that it is spirituality incognito.

In the phrase 'sex drives', is the word 'drives' a noun or a verb? Certainly sex is a great hunger, a powerful energy, and it can be an intense delight. But sexual activity can be the occasion of withering rather than healing, of tragedy rather than comedy, of pain rather than pleasure. Sometimes it is a mixture of these things, satisfaction and yearning experienced together. And in an atmosphere of relaxation and trust it can hint at the divine comedy itself.

What is abundantly clear is that it is about something more than biological reproduction. Of course, in a biological sense, it *is* primarily about the continuation of the species, but if it were only this, we should have to say that it had nothing to do with our humanity, as distinct from our being part of the animal world. However, we do experience our sexuality and sexual relationships as having to do with our uniqueness. My sexuality pervades and permeates my unique being: I sense it as inextricably bound up with my identity as a person. If that is so with myself, it will become even more so as I express my need for others, and more particularly for a specific other. Solo sex may be pleasurable, but it leaves an awareness of how much better it would be with someone else. Further, my sexuality is bound up with the relationships that have done much to form me, with parents and the community around, with all their ambiguities. Because it is so easy to be hurt in the groin, physically and emotionally, it is precisely there that we seek affirmation – acceptance and sustenance – as flesh-body persons. Lastly, my sexuality seems to evoke not only my

need for another human being, but also my need for The
Other. There is always a beyondness that seems to beckon in
and through our sexuality and sexual relationships, and sex
never yields all that it promises of creativity and communion.
It can give much more than we usually anticipate or experience, but the desire always remains for something less broken,
less partial, less temporary. And that seems to be true to the
experience of even the best of marriages.

If sex and sexuality cannot be separated from our identity,
our relationships, and our faith, they are likely to gather to
themselves a number of metaphors and associations. So do we
attempt to make some sense of this bewildering power.

'Health' is one such association. Because emotional wounds
and compulsive behaviour are the stuff of their business,
counsellors will often ask, "What needs healing in this
person's sexuality?" But it is worth asking another question,
"Do we interpret sexuality too much in terms of disease and
healing?" The question is serious – witness the way in which
the medical profession has taken over as the expert. We want
doctors to use technological skill and to give sound medical
advice, but do we want them as decision makers *for* us, and
guardians of our morals? Contraception, abortion, childbirth,
same-sex relationships – doctors are often perceived as the
most significant seat of authority. They may not all want that
role, even if it is easy for doctor and patient to collude with the
expectation. What other voices should we listen to when trying
to answer the question, What makes for a 'healthy' sex life?
Who should make decisions as to how we live as flesh-body
beings?

Another association is 'duty'. Indeed, the word 'purity'
links the notion of duty with that of health – pure minds and
healthy genes in the transmission of life and culture to the next
generation. And in the religion of good works sex becomes a
duty to one's spouse, one's country, and one's God, with
procreation its only purpose. Mixed in with this attitude is
often a fervent and unthinking brand of patriotism (sometimes

backed by an ecclesiastical authority), and a restriction of women to the three roles of child-bearing, cooking, and church-going – the German 'Kinder, Küche, Kirche'. Duty is connected with the conviction that society should operate in an orderly and law-abiding way, a conviction that should always override all other considerations. Sex in this view seems to threaten anarchy.

If you associate sex with issues of health and duty, it is probably hard to associate it with 'pleasure'. Of course the kind of pleasure that declines into a compulsion to have one's desires met immediately – the caricature of the so-called permissive society – becomes a form of cruelty. Nevertheless, pleasure is one of the characteristics of the mature life of faith, however uneasy Christians have been about it. We occasionally talk of heavenly banquets and enjoyable suppers, but the ecstasies of the flesh? Most religiously inclined people have lost touch with the value of the material, and the thought of God smiling when human beings are enjoying sexual ecstasy can sound shocking. But a Christian understanding of matter, of material stuff, takes it as God-given, and at the heart of Christian worship it is said that bread and wine have some *body*, *somebody*, in them.

The commitment of love, with its lasting concern for the welfare of the other, is the container that makes pleasure safe and relaxing. The greater the trust, the more satisfying the pleasure. And I don't think it far-fetched to draw a comparison between the making of love and the making of Eucharist. Perhaps the one reflects the other, the one a personal focus, the other a corporate focus, for the generating of love in the world. After all, at the heart of each are the statements, of person to person, and of God to the community of persons, "You matter to me", and "I am willing to die for you", ie. grace and sacrifice. Love is bound up with the physicality of sex and the physicality of bread. The attempt to ignore this turns love into a shadow of itself.

Our sexuality, then, is full of intricacy and complexity. It is the stuff both of being stuck *and* of our growth in freedom. Consequently, it is inevitably bound up with anything we may want to say about spirituality.

Spirituality is nothing less than the whole of life orientated towards God, shaped by God, graced by God. That *includes* the sexuality of each individual and the sexuality of all, in our personal and corporate desire to come together and to create. So it may be more accurate to talk of a spirituality *of* sexuality, sexuality in the light of the Love of God, being transformed by the Spirit at work within and among us.

Spirituality is not an inward-looking, self-regarding cultivation of the 'soul', in the sense of a supposed detached part of a person, uninfluenced by the 'body' which it is inhabiting as its temporary home. 'Soul' is not a 'thing', rather is it the movement of the whole being under the pressure of life's contradictions and in the relaxation of life's celebrations. Such movement is also bound up with the movement of the universe: spirituality is therefore inevitably concerned with my neighbour and with planet earth.

Some people try to deny either sexuality or spirituality. This results in spiritism or materialism, each refusing to acknowledge the reality of the other. Others try to oppose the one to the other, which is dualism. Such -isms do reflect our experience of often being split in two, but beyond the split is the possibility of reconciliation and harmony, even if the cost is the struggle and tension of seeking to hold the two together in a creative way. We may think that 'ways of making love' comes more easily under the heading of sexuality, and 'ways of praying' more easily under the heading of spirituality, but they cannot so easily be prised apart in experience, however much each will have its typical features, practices, symbols, and rituals. Always one will affect the other – the art of touch is not unaffected by the art of solitude, nor the quality of solitude unaffected by the quality of touch.

So I want to claim that the roots of Godwardness are in matter, flesh and blood, material stuff, earth; they are not to be rejected, however painful our experience of them might be. Our sexuality is fundamental to our lives, both through delight and through contradiction. The further we pursue the questions which are raised by our sexuality, the more we are made aware of the profoundest movements of our being. Through our experience of sexuality there is the possibility of our becoming more open to the Beyond whom we call God.

3
Making connections

IF we cannot make a complete distinction between the sexual and the spiritual, neither can we between the private and the public. There *are* connections to be made, however much we like to pretend that sexuality belongs to the privacy of our bedrooms. Now there is a certain privacy which is to be respected. Intimacy can be betrayed. We are appalled if private letters have to be read out in a court of law. I remember feeling uneasy when some houses down the street where I lived were being demolished and the wallpaper of a bedroom was revealed to the public eye. It is not for nothing that we use the phrase 'private parts' in public discourse. We find it hard to decide just how much sex education should be taught in the semi-public classroom. And it is certainly difficult to speak and write of what is private without cheapening ourselves and those close to us.

Yet nothing that we do, however legitimately private the action, takes place in a social vacuum. Every relationship is influenced by our common *membership* of the *body politic*. When a husband and wife are in bed together, it is said that there are four other people present, not an angel at each corner, but the father and mother of each partner. The influence of the previous generation is profound on the next, shaping both our attitudes towards making love and also the quality of that lovemaking. The parents themselves may have found it hard to think of sex as anything but an unwelcome mechanism for having children, and even if they have *talked* differently with their offspring, the emotional power of how *they* were brought up will have its repercussions – even to the third and fourth generations.

It is not my intention here to look in detail at the myriad issues involved. I simply want to illustrate the point that any spirituality of sexuality must take into account the complexities of the corporate life of a society. On any one issue a book could be written, and in practice the working through of personal dilemmas will need to take into account a lot of detail. And that is my first point. The *detail* of the facts and circumstances of such dilemmas, of the motives of the people involved, and of the likely consequences of different courses of action, takes spirituality out of an otherworldly atmosphere and links it firmly with the morality of corporate and personal relationships, which in turn is inextricably linked with issues of law, justice, and the common good. To understand that point clearly, you have only to read a Hebrew prophet like Amos. In Christian terms this respect for the detail of life is a way of honouring the Incarnation, God becoming human, flesh and blood, in a particular place at a particular time, as a member of a particular religious community, and living under a particular political regime.

For example, the fact of easily available contraceptive devices is neither simple nor neutral. Condoms and pills have had complex practical and moral implications. They have caused anguish of decision-making for generations of human beings, and at the same time have released women from the almost inevitable connection between sex and conception. I do not know how much guilt is still around amongst Roman Catholic couples who practise artificial contraception whilst being aware of but ignoring the Church's ruling against the practice. One commentator did try and argue that if the intention of every sexual act is openness to life, this could mean being open to an enhanced quality of life and love between the two people concerned as well as meaning open to conception. I suspect such a distinction is too subtle for it to have much effect. But there is clearly a struggle, a public debate and public declarations affecting private hopes and guilts, and a long history of deep emotional response to what has been perceived as an artificial and unwarranted interference with the course of nature – and there is a complex philosophical debate hidden in that last phrase!

Again, what has been happening to the spirituality of women who now exercise choice about child-bearing? Processes of scientific research have given the opportunity of a shift from sex as primarily about procreation to sex as primarily about the quality of the relationship. I can remember hearing of a couple who married in the 1920s who had sexual intercourse only when they wanted to have children. Otherwise the relationship was asexual. Presumably the occasions of their sexual lovemaking were few. So what difference does it make to human beings in a relationship when there are in fact thousands of such occasions?

We have recently seen another shift in the public domain relating to private behaviour, with discussions and advertisements on television about condoms as a means of protection against sexually transmitted diseases, especially the transmission of HIV III. Fear, protection, and caution have become part of the social sexual climate. Restraint comes to the fore again as a virtue extolled rather than muted. People worry about whether spreading knowledge about condoms will seem to encourage fleeting sexual contacts. Human societies have always to some extent sought to control sexual behaviour through laws, to give a framework to a desire that can be so overwhelming as to result in anarchic and destructive behaviour. But there is an extreme which is intolerable in any society which values even a measure of freedom and of personal choice. In any case, control can never be absolute. What we have experienced over the last couple of generations is some loosening of that control, followed in the last year or two by a reaction that seeks to tighten it again. But the fact and the know-how of contraception will hardly go away, and this puts pressure on human beings to exercise their sense of responsibility in a deliberate and heightened way. Greater knowledge always implies that. But the less we exercise that responsibility personally, the greater the danger of other kinds of technology being used to impose control. Using knowledge to advance wisdom is a deeply spiritual task.

Here is another example. A whole history of a culture, of attitudes of law, medicine, and religion is bound up in the controversy as to whether and how same-sex relationships should be part of sex education in schools. What information does a young person glean about a phenomenon that is not talked about, yet partially known about, often with distortions and through the filters of prejudice? What picture lies behind the opinion that 'homosexuality' should not be 'promoted'? It sounds like suspicion of an advertising campaign that should at least be forced to add a government health warning. And if there is a moral distinction between gang rape and a long-term lesbian relationship, either of which could be in a person's mind when 'homosexuality' is mentioned, what exactly do people think is being 'promoted'? The point again is that a phrase in a parliamentary bill is a public matter concerning private behaviour and knowledge of the same: the force of law is being invoked to stop anything but a negative view of certain kinds of sexual relationship. There is a clash between those whose perspective and experience leads them to fear that people could be converted to or trapped by what is perceived as an alien way of life and those whose perspective and experience leads them to claim that a person *discovers* a same-sex orientation that has been dormant, perhaps by the occasion of falling in love for the first time, whether at 15 or 50. Emotions run high, an indication that the truth about the issue is not open and clear for most people, some being afraid of public debate and others pressing for it. But it is obvious that we are faced with something much more than simply what consenting adults do in private. Their spirituality is being shaped by all manner of influences in the wider world. In legal terms, it will make quite a difference to the atmosphere of a society if the age of consent is 21, 18, 16, 15 or 50 (all of which are on the statute books of various countries) or indeed if the law has no age of consent at all. In medical terms, it will make quite a difference if a person's behaviour is classified as neurotic or healthy. In religious terms, the degree of guilt and shame

about a sexual relationship will largely depend on the serious-
ness with which a person takes the teaching of a particular
Church, as well as on the actual content of that teaching. The
impression given by a gay psychotherapist in France who is a
Quaker is likely to be different from that of a heterosexual
fundamentalist psychotherapist in the southern states of
America. And if a human being's sexuality is not recognized by
the society around, a dark enclosed closet will not exactly
encourage the breathing of a free spirit. Some fling open those
doors when they can, others submit to the doors being locked
from the outside and then add another lock on the inside. A
sense of inner freedom can doubtless grow in any prison, but
that is no reason for injustice, the kind of injustice that was
suffered by thousands of homosexually orientated people in
the concentration camps of Nazi Germany.

There is one further connection between private and public
that I want to mention, that which concerns the link between
sexuality and the profoundest issues of our day, issues of
violence and war, racism and ecology. Does a technology that
so often asserts itself *over against* nature, rather than *co-operates
with* nature, arise out of an unchecked masculine desire to be
the successful hunter of prey and the heroic vanquisher of
enemies? If we deny the erotic, if we suppress the tender, if we
exclude the feminine from appropriate power, is not the result
hatred and violence? A saint can wax lyrical about the
ecstasies of 'spiritual' love unconnected with the flesh, as did
Bernard of Clairvaux, yet dread sex and hate infidels and
heretics. By contrast, I gather that the various native peoples
of the Arctic are very affirming of sex and have no words for
war.

In popular mythology, white woman is often pictured as
pure and delicate, the archetypal virgin and mother, while
black woman is animal, to be exploited by white man for sex
and labour. Black man on the other hand is pictured as a
ravenous sexual beast who must be kept in bounds if not in
chains, and who has been loaded with the white man's

unacknowledged powerful sexual desires and guilt. There is a strong emotional current here which helped to sustain slavery in America, is part of the apartheid system in South Africa, and infects racist Britain. What white person in this country does not need to eradicate the prejudice that the white man's 'mind' is superior and the black man's 'body' has a physical energy to be feared?

Alongside this racist myth are those distorted perceptions of disabled people and of Jewish people as grotesque (the disabled are thought to have no sexuality and are symbolically castrated by a refusal to recognize their needs. Jewish men are circumcised and so thought to be sexually different). We are not far from scapegoating whole groups of people out of an unacknowledged and unaccepted (because seemingly unacceptable) depth of sexual emotion and desire in those whose power is won at the very expense of keeping openness about such matters at bay. Such has been 'Christian' Europe's all too frequent attitude towards black, Jew, disabled, and gay, an attitude that can be traced through many a respected British novelist earlier this century and that reached virulent and climactic expression in the Nazi policy of extermination.

Maybe worst of all, we are beginning to reap the consequences of our masculine rape of the earth herself. We have forgotten, and are only beginning to remember, the wiser relationship of kinship with the earth and a serious responsibility as stewards of our planet. Is the white male macho technocrat, whether farmer, businessman, or politician, dominating government and media, a singularly dangerous species?

If these dimensions of the body politic and body sexual are significant – and I should be surprised if reading this chapter has not evoked strong thoughts and feelings – they are part of what comes under the heading of spirituality. Sexual issues are part of the corporate reality of our spiritual concerns, that the kingdoms of this world should be transformed into the kingdom – or is it commonwealth? – of Christ, with its vision of a world drawn towards and shaped by the divine will and purpose. The issues that I have sketched are not just abstract ones for intellectual discussion, but are part of the stuff of human beings' agonies and joys, their relationships and decisions, through which their character is formed, both as individuals and as communities.

Such matter, such stuff, is the material, the earthy material, the only material that we know of: how then can earth be hallowed, flesh transfigured?

THEME CHART

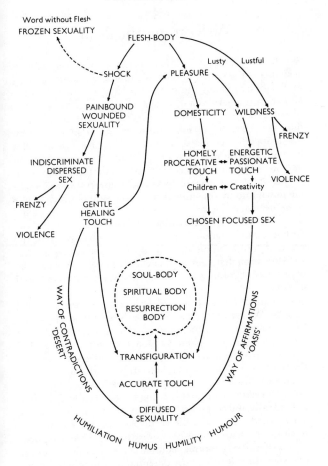

Ways to the Transfiguration of Flesh-Body Sexuality

4
Welcoming the flesh

So the starting-point for a consideration of a spirituality of sexuality is the reality of the flesh, of material stuff, of being matter-of-fact about the facts of matter, of holding to the Christian conviction that matter does matter. The word for 'flesh' in the New Testament is 'sarx': it is a neutral word, and does not, contrary to some subsequent Christian thought, automatically have negative associations. The flesh in itself is not bad. It is true that exclusive concentration on the flesh, on its own, in isolation, distorts a person, for the flesh is subject to the inevitable processes of decay and disintegration, of breaking down into its constituent parts, the sum of which is less than the whole. Therefore, we are not to set our hearts on the flesh, for that is to be drawn into the spiral of decay. But the flesh is not to be ignored, denied, beaten down. It can be the place of transformation if it is open to something greater working through it, moving it towards a more complex whole, occasionally becoming radiant, often raw, yet the raw material of glory.

We cannot escape from the flesh, however ambivalent it may be. We certainly experience our sexuality in the flesh – there is no other place to experience it. It is in the flesh that we know pleasure and pain, passion and hurt, ecstasy and tenderness, in the flow of fluids, of blood, of juices, of semen, of the flow of life-blood, of future life growing within.

Further, 'flesh-body' is the recognizable form of the person I am, as I relate as an earthly being to others as flesh-bodies, individually and corporately. As flesh-body I am and I move on the earth, as part of the earth. As a person I cannot be separated from flesh-body before death, though what happens to me as flesh-body may make of me a being who is degenerating into something less than my potential or who is being transfigured into something beyond my wildest imaginings. But this something beyond, this something potentially greater, is not an entity untouched by flesh and called a 'soul', but my very self at the deepest level of my being, battered, delighted, wrenched apart, lured, seduced, and most profoundly loved, a person becoming recognizable, maybe, as 'soul-body'.

As flesh-body I operate in several ways – physically, mentally, emotionally, imaginatively. Sometimes, I focus on one, sometimes on another, sometimes in combination. Through the whole process, through the whole of my being-that-is-becoming, operates my '*will*-ingness', my capacity to be 'en-*heart*-ened', the ability to set my compass Godward, open to passion, warmth, gentleness, care, through which experience I blossom and become open to transfiguration. However, I may refuse to set my compass, I may allow it to drift, at that deep level, 'un-*will*-ingly', 'dis-*heart*-ened'. If I do this, I shall be on the way to disintegration, closed in on flesh-body alone, denying any other reality.

So flesh-body is not the perfect place to be, it is not yet 'heaven', but it is good enough, and might afford us more pleasure and less pain if we could accept that fact. But do we actually believe that flesh-body is good enough, that the expression of flesh-body sexually is good? Do we feel even partially at home in the flesh? I forget who asked this question, but I think the answer we give will be revealing: "After making love, do you feel that you have had a bath, or that you need one?"

I would go on to ask other questions, not traditionally to be found in manuals of self-examination. What Anglo-Saxon words do you use for sexual intercourse – especially if you are a man reading this? Are they hard, battering, mechanical words? Do you know, by way of contrast, the old English word 'swive'? (You can find it in Chaucer.) Do you know what it is to tune into your own and your partner's physical rhythms, riding the waves in an erotic dance?

The contrast I have in mind is rather like the difference between two kinds of swimming pool: one is rectangular, with lines drawn on the bottom of the pool, and designed for serious exercise, for competitions and achievement; the other is more like a pond, with curving edges, and perhaps a machine for creating waves, and slides that land you in the water with a pleasant splash, and subtropical plants decorating the edges. It is designed for fun, for play and enjoyment.

Does an inner voice ever say about sexual intercourse, "This is taking too much time; let's get it over with"? Behind that voice does there not lurk an unspoken rejection of the flesh, almost disgust? Is physical sexual activity an experience of the whole flesh-body, or are sensations limited to the genital area?

Sex in the dunes is beautiful in the advertisements, but they don't tell you that the sand gets everywhere. Are you offended by that sentence or do you laugh? On seeing a helicopter flying above on coastal patrol, partner A mutters, 'Damn', and reaches for a towel, while partner B turns over, waves, and blows the pilot a kiss.

Do you regard solo sex as self-abuse, masturbation, or being kind to yourself? I am told that Gaelic has no word as such for masturbation, but people use the euphemism, 'your friendly hand'. June Singer even suggests that solo sex can be a symbol of our own inner wholeness and independence as individuals, and that a sexual relationship then becomes a matter of choice rather than of desperate need. I suspect that most of us look at the process of maturing the other way round: it is through our relationships that some of our deep needs are met and we begin to find our way to wholeness. But the point here is that it is unlikely that we shall ever before have come across such a positive statement about masturbation. Are you uneasy? If so, why?

And what did a priest mean by saying that he found preaching the most erotic activity he knew? Is eroticism in worship misplaced, or is most preaching wrapped up in the head? Do not the best preachers use, in the broadest sense, their emotional and sexual energies as one of the means of communicating to their congregations?

James Nelson writes of participating in Midnight Mass at Christmas in King's College Chapel in Cambridge. He was overwhelmed by the sensuousness of the architecture, the candles, and the music, and the golds and reds and blues of Rubens' painting, *The Adoration of the Magi*, above the altar, with the Magi yearning towards the figure of the infant Jesus. He found himself sexually aroused when receiving communion. Dare we, at that point, praise God, saying, "The Word was made flesh: alleluia!"?

5
Desiring affirmation

EVERYTHING you need to know about God but were always afraid to ask is conveyed in and through flesh-body. Incarnation is a fleshly and sexual doctrine. Flesh-body receives the highest affirmation through the divine presence becoming clear to us, being revealed to us, not *in* but *as* flesh. Flesh is a *means* of human loving, not an obstacle to it.

That thought is all the more awesome when we realize that the Incarnation did not wait until human wisdom and tenderness had become mature enough for an unreserved welcome. Indeed, the flesh is too much a place of contradictions for that, with sin and pain inextricably bound up with it. The human response to Incarnation was bound to be mixed. The grace and truth of this enfleshed being, Jesus of Nazareth, affirmed and accepted the delight and beauty of the flesh, and at the same time knew that hidden resentments about flesh that had been hurt would focus in a brooding spirit of revenge that would harm and kill. But the seeds of the hope of a fuller affirmation were sown, and men and women since have yearned for its flowering.

Yes, the language of flesh-body is partial and broken. Nevertheless it is the best we have for understanding God. This is not to say that, as a matter of fact and a fact of matter, any and every human relationship *automatically* reveals God, but it is to say that there is no better place to look if you are searching. The clue to the meaning of the word 'God' is to be found in the sexual-fleshy, not detached from that reality. The flesh-body is *intrinsic* to our capacity for love. When the prophet Hosea heard these words of God, "I will betroth you to myself, to have and to hold, and you will *know* the Lord," he was using a bodily metaphor – the relationship of people to God will be sexually consummated. (Hosea 1.9) The language implies that at the very least the hoped-for relationship with

God will be even *more* bodily binding than a human sexual relationship.

The sexual flesh-body can be the place of the revelation of the sacred. It does not need topping up with a 'sacrament' to make it sacred. It is already sacramental, a means of grace when received in faith and trust and obedience. All that a Sacrament with a capital 'S' can do as a ritual is to remind, focus, articulate, give depth to, celebrate the ordinary daily sacraments, the reverent handling of matter, drawing them further into the mystery we call God and saving what is already sacramental from degenerating into meaningless sign or boring idolatry. We do not 'make love' in any more sacred a manner by thinking of God while we are doing it: our activity has to be wholehearted and singleminded and wholebodied if it is to be godly.

Dietrich Bonhoeffer, in one of his letters from prison, wryly remarked that it was at the very least 'bad taste', more importantly an attempt to be more pious than God, for a husband to be thinking of heaven while in his wife's arms. He was concerned there, and in other places in his writings, to affirm the value of what *is* in the secular and everyday. When that includes a great happiness, the attempt to bring in God, as it were from the wings, actually detracts from the deeply *spiritual* character of that experience. In any case, is it not God who is being celebrated, however incognito?

It is hard for those who are 'spiritually' minded, 'meaning' minded, to grasp this. If your 'head' is too much in the clouds, to come down to earth, to drop into 'flesh' and 'heart', may well feel like falling into an abyss, rather than coming home. We are all somewhat split and afraid, finding it hard to believe that our sexuality is indeed *God*-given, *God's* way of bringing us close to one another, as we reach out, touch, and embrace.

6
Hating the flesh

For many people, the statements of the previous chapter and the explicitness of the one before it will have painted a picture that is far from their experience. At best the words will have seemed like statements of faith by someone of a different creed. For flesh-body may have been experienced in such a painful way that there has been a turning away from anything to do with sexuality. A defensive attitude may have developed, a guarded neutrality, with watchful suspicion. At worst, sex may seem tainted with evil or contorted with agony. Some have denied its reality altogether, by unconscious repression. Others have taken revenge on their fellow human beings, making murderous rape on other flesh-bodies, even infecting others with the virus that can lead to AIDS. They experience nothing but a weird and ghastly short-lived excitement and a constant murmur of deep dissatisfaction.

If you have received a severe flesh-body shock, years back in an infancy you can now barely remember, you may well have frozen your sexual feelings. You now want word *without* flesh, grace *without* carnality. If you are aware of the hurt that was done to you, you may have some feeling, but it is likely to be a cold hatred spurred into action by deep-seated and irrational guilt. Flesh-body must now be hated, it must submit. Life is lived above the navel, preferably above the neck. Is it a coincidence that clergy began to wear dog collars in the later part of the nineteenth century, that band round the neck that cuts off the rest of flesh-body from communication with the head? Perhaps I jest, but who was it that said that sex on the brain is the worst place to have it? (That is parallel, I suppose, to a religion of credal formulae – it's the worst place to believe it.)

A person who lives too much in the head may experience life as no more than a succession of unintegrated thoughts,

haunted by sex and by 'God', disembodied, disenchanted by
the flesh, with no body-language, not even a few 'words' in
what will feel like a foreign tongue, certainly not enough to
communicate with another person. It is likely that sexual
activity will be experienced as a devouring of parts, seeking
something that cannot be gained that way, rather than a
sharing of the whole person. Sexual energy is then dispersed
and sexual activity indiscriminate, a cycle of dust-and-ashes
sex, with the lurking desire to be rid of it altogether. One of the
'fathers' of the Church, Origen, went so far as to castrate
himself of such an unruly member.

An inability either to enjoy or to endure the flesh can result
in a kind of stratospheric loving, not exactly empty of meaning,
but beyond the atmosphere of human flesh in a realm of so-
called 'ideas'. I remember a mathematics scholar once who
wished he could be a 'pure idea', so problematic did he find life
as flesh-body being. In religious circles, some 'gurus' have
been both sexually promiscuous and productive of a succession of promiscuous (ie. indiscriminate and unrelated)
'wise sayings', evoking an enraptured, "Isn't that beautiful?"
from his followers. This is dangerously near the sentimentality
about sex and religion, the reverse side of which coin is cruelty:
it is never far from violent, violating sex.

We see a different kind of separation of sex from religion in
some adolescents, whose difficulties with sex are left behind
(for a while) in favour of religious fervour. An ecstatic 'Jesus,
O Jesus' can sound like an impending orgasm. We may readily
admit that a desire for God has sexual roots, but where this is
unacknowledged, the resultant split divides into a loathing of
the flesh and a hate-filled religion, uneasy before God and
violent towards neighbour. This is why the New Testament, in
the First Letter of John, is insistent that we cannot be
Christians unless we acknowledge that Jesus came *in the flesh*.

Estranged from flesh-body, strangers to ourselves, we
become hateful: we project that hatred on to others, in the rape
of other human beings, women or men, in the rape of the earth,

in the attempt to exterminate (or exile or quarantine) any people who remind us of what is unresolved in ourselves.

Out of his experience of the concentration camp of Auschwitz, the Italian writer Primo Levi reflected on how deep is this unconscious conviction that the stranger is inevitably an enemy who must be violently opposed. Most of the time the conviction is indeed hidden, like a latent lethal virus, but occasionally it erupts in sporadic and unconnected acts of violence and violation. On rare occasions there can be an epidemic, as in Germany in the thirties. Such hatred then becomes *the* characteristic of a whole regime, and the end of the chain of logic was the death camps. We should shudder that the virus is still alive and active.

Sexual energy on the loose is no different. It becomes wild and frenzied and violent, resulting in rape and murder, or it becomes steady and cool and hateful, resulting in systematic killing. This is the place to locate the devilish in sex, flesh without word, carnality without grace. At its centre is a lie and hardness of heart.

(Umberto Eco has one of his characters in *The Name of the Rose* assert that the Devil is not the Prince of Matter but is that humourless arrogance that presumes to know the truth and is unaffected by doubt.)

This is 'masculine body' on the loose, body as machine: you screw with your tool. You read your 'owner's manual' to improve your prowess and your potency. You must win in the competition of size of weapon and number of conquests. In the initiation ceremony of the all-male group, the new entrant may be humiliated, dominated, even treated 'as a woman' before being elevated to the status of a man. The erotic may be allowed, in sexual humiliation, as long as it is never named.

Many women do not need to read of such initiation ceremonies to know the effect of 'masculine body' on the loose. It seems that we are still stuck with the ancient thought that the man is associated with intellect and rational power, imposing his will on the woman, whose wild sexuality is deemed to be disordered and must be subdued. In one myth, Zeus gave birth to Athena from his brain.

If masculine dominance and feminine submission is the name of the game, what has happened to mutuality? If sensation is limited to penis and vagina, what has happened to the glow of sensation through the whole flesh-body? If the aggressive male forces the female to fight or flee or freeze, what has happened to the dance, the dance in which each contributes a powerful but loving energy? If size and potency face weakness, what has happened to the weakness in men and the strength in women? If we have tools to work with and stuff to be worked on, what has happened to play? If men are haunted by the urge to perform and achieve, and women by duty and the fear of failure, what has happened to pleasure and relaxation?

Rilke in the third of his letters describes such male-dominated sexuality as all 'rouse and restlessness', with balloon-like pomp and narrow-minded prejudice obscuring and distorting love, and making it feel a heavy burden rather than mutual delight.

Such is sexual activity that arises out of shock, pain, repressed hurt, deflecting desire out of the direction of creativity, union, and the sym-bolic, and towards destruction, separation, and the dia-bolic. Its re-direction is by means of delving what might be termed the Way of Contradictions. After examining that, we shall return to the more positive way, the Way of Affirmations, the way that most of us have not, thank God, entirely lost, and whose keyword is pleasure.

7
Recovering tenderness

LET us suppose that violence and coercion are absent from a particular sexual encounter. Let us also suppose that the two parties are adult and consenting. The action may be indiscriminate and the sexual energy dispersed rather than used to build love into the relationship, but for a few moments tension is released and loneliness relieved. Now no one would pretend that such satisfaction can be anything more than minimal. Indeed, a person may find the compulsive element in the repetition of that kind of encounter to be depressing and humiliating. For some, there may not be much choice about such patterns of behaviour: it is possible for sex to become an addiction. What is good in itself can become inordinate and destructive in practice because it is out of proportion with the rest of a person's life. Self-hatred may be the root. But to rage against such behaviour is to increase the power of such hatred – and it is to ignore the hints of something better that are experienced even in the midst of what feels largely unsatisfactory. Indeed a person may be blind to most of those better things in store, may not have sufficient vision of them to desire to change. But those hints of goodness should make us draw back from the assertion that God is totally absent from such attempts at loving. Is not God the encourager of the good and the bearer of the hurt consequent on our destructiveness? Might it not be that God, in strange and seemingly contradictory ways, is driving a person into a desert place, there to be challenged to strive with all that is chaotic within and in relationship, and at the same time to be aware of the presence of angels, an awareness that encourages that person not to succumb to despair, to the lie that God is no longer present?

For deserts are *monotonous* places, sand dune after sand dune, where one's sense of direction is easily lost. 'Desert' sex could be described as mechanically repetitive, going nowhere, with a short-circuiting of energy, producing nothing creative and vanishing into sterile sand. It is also the place of pornography: one-dimensional sex, concentrating on parts, using the other as an object, with hatred of the flesh hovering as the demon. The contrast is with the erotic: complex, multi-dimensional, the other as a person with whom enjoyment is mutual. This is art, pervaded by a love of the flesh.

The desert can also be a *monstrous* place, of sandstorms and howling wind: 'desert' sex is on the loose in the psyche, making a person prone to illusions and lies, tending towards a taking of one's pleasure without thought for the other, with violence lurking in the wings. The power of sex is still not integrated with the rest of the personality: it is detached and overweening. There may be minimal good, but it can be no more than minimal and even that is often obscured.

The desert, then, is the place of lustfulness and painfulness, of frenzy and fury. The question is, Can the Furies be faced, acknowledged, striven with, so that, as in the myth, they become the Eumenides, the Bearers of Grace? For neither the monotonous nor the monstrous yield the beauty of the desert, the moment of *monstrance*, of showing, of revelation. That comes in softer moments, in the light of dawn or sunset. For what is missing in the repetition of the monotonous and the frenzy of the monstrous, is tenderness. Masud Khan asks somewhere where excitement will stop once the taboo, the restraint, of tenderness is removed.

For some, their intrinsic trust in the tenderness of touch has been violated early on, and they were driven into the desert, and they have always found it hard to believe that God could be there in the power of love to bring them home. Trust in the flesh-body was harmed by body-shock. From such a trauma there is no easy recovery. The shock that freezes may have come from no touch at all, or from too much touch, either of violence or of possessiveness – which is a kind of violence too, a holding too close when a respectful distance is needed. Such a shock can be almost too much for the infant. The organism finds it impossible to cope, and the experience, along with the pain, is repressed.

The shock may be so severe that it is 'touch and go' whether an infant chooses life or death. And even if it is not as severe as that, even if the freezing is partial, flesh-body has very early on become associated with pain and not with pleasure. In adult life, sexuality becomes trapped in a cycle of desire and withdrawal, repetition and frenzy. Sexually, 'touch and go' is precisely the way of dispersal. It is not easy to 'touch and stay', so that après-sex is not 'tristesse' but 'joie'.

The quest is to recover enough trust in a human being precisely to touch and be touched and not to freeze – nor to flee or fight when the pain begins to be felt. Perhaps we need to recover a practice of 'firm tenderness' with one another, a broad dimension of our sexuality that is neither flabby nor sentimental on the one hand, nor too strong and energetic on the other. This is not a widely known part of the grammar of body language, and it may be that we have to learn it anew with all the stumbling of childhood. At any one moment each of us answers a set of questions in a particular way, and we need these answers to be respected by others: how close do I want another to come? how distant? how high or low are my boundaries? what quality of touch do I need? If an approach by another is too overwhelming, too frequent, too soon, too sudden, the self as flesh-body will repel the invader, will 'expel the foreign body'. Even if the approach is caring, it may still be experienced as too explosive. (Perhaps this is why we fear that death will be a painful dislocation rather than a gentle transition into a new kind of life – do we trust that there is the guiding hand of Love?)

Certainly we feel the pressure of these questions in our day. For we live in melting-pots, in a mobile mixture of cultures and peoples and faiths and relationships. What *are* the appropriate boundaries in a world of blood transfusions, transplants, international travel, and the international virus?

We need a delicate sense of discrimination. For along with

appropriate touch there is the need in each of us for appropriate space. We need a delicate touch because it is so easy for a withdrawal, a slight distancing, to be experienced by the other as a rejection, resulting in further pain. By contrast, too insistent an approach can feel suffocating, and the other withdraws within. Few of us have become wise in these ways of loving.

But the need is urgent for the right kind, the bearable kind, of closeness, the beginnings of an understanding of a new flesh-body language in which to hear afresh the wonderful works of God. Is this the middle ground for the carer and counsellor – neither all words and no touch in any circumstances, nor supposedly 'therapeutic' sexual touch?

Could this kind of discerning contact be the 'non-possessive warmth' of firm, gentle touch? Could it be the 'accurate empathy' of appropriate touch? Could it be the 'genuineness' that comes from a thorough understanding of the language of touch and a using of it to free rather than to dominate, to be truthful rather than manipulative? Here could be a healing touch, a meeting in its own way of flesh-body persons, each encounter alive and unique.

Touch would have its own meaning. It would not be without meaning, all over the place, nor ritualised out of all meaning – into a mere handshake or peck on the cheek. The rigidity and tension of the wounded, the frozen, and the frenzied, would subside into a relaxed contentment. There would be the sense of dropping out of the fear that is characterized by short, sharp, shallow breathing into the security of long, even, deep breathing. It could lead to a diffused experience of sexuality, the sexuality of the entire flesh-body broadly felt in every touch, a slow surrendering to the goodness of the flesh. It could ease a person out of the fears of drowning or of suffocation, through the frozenness of body-shock, the ice slowly melting. It would be a gentle sexualizing, slowly nearing the point of being able to contain the forces of passion, its explosiveness no longer being too much, no longer the occasion of a further springing apart.

Such a process cannot be easy or quick. Patterns of compulsion are not easily changed. Shame and guilt about dispersed sex are often exaggerated, but powerful for all that. Solemnity lends extra power to the habit. To pretend that an action is worse than it is feeds distortion and the motor of repetition. It leads to that inordinate self-hatred and punishment that easily gets projected on to others. It is surely more mature to acknowledge calmly both the inevitability of much of what we do – how much freedom to choose do most of us realistically have? – and the fact that it is less than the best, or even less than a possible good – less than what we want, and what, in our best moments, we glimpse.

The process of becoming more free is long and difficult. Sometimes the only choice seems to be in the kind of pain. But it will involve daring to be still, daring to become more aware, to look, to contemplate. It will mean looking in detail at what we do. It will mean feeling through the shame, the humiliation, the fear, the anger, the grief. It will mean embracing those feelings as our own, being kind to ourselves in the process, staying with the pain of the contradictions of what is unresolved, putting more *body* into sexual desire and feeling, and even sinning – if that is the right word – boldly. Then the vision grows within of something better. Laughter begins to bubble up, even at the memories of our stupidities. After all, flesh-bodies together are not pathetic or athletic or grotesque, but ordinary and *funny*. We begin to breathe and move and feel more freely, flowering into a flowing sensuousness. We are on the verge of play and pleasure. It is use-less really, like the uselessness, the play, the pleasure, of worship – or is that too a solemn duty?

When we play, we cannot hurry: we need to take time out of time and to become unaware of the passing of time. This may be the only way in which we can begin to trust that the other will not wound us. Jack Nichols writes in *Men's Liberation* that such play can enable us to relax enough to become vulnerable, and not to be afraid of it but to enjoy it.

So our experience of sexuality as a spiritual journey is one that brings us from coldness to passion, from dumbness to speech, from frozenness to movement, from sensation in the extremities to sensation through the entire flesh-body. And it can all happen even in the middle years:

"He brought light out of darkness, not out of a lesser light; he can bring thy summer out of winter, though thou have no spring; though in the ways of fortune, or understanding, or conscience, thou have benighted till now, wintered and frozen, clouded and eclipsed, damped and benummed, smothered and stupefied until now, now God comes to thee, not as in the dawning of the day, not as in the bud of spring, but as the sun at noon to illustrate all shadows, as the sheaves in harvest, to fill all penuries, all occasions invite his mercies, and all times are his seasons." So John Donne preached in St. Paul's Cathedral on Christmas Day in 1624.

8
Discovering pleasure

THE concerns of a spirituality of sexuality include the experience of passionate pleasure, the passion of energy, excitement, and thrill, the pleasure of swiving, making love, melting in delight. These things can be good and godly. Alan Watts wrote in *Nature, Man and Woman* that such sexuality has its own glow that spreads through all relationships, while becoming intensely radiant at certain points.

Is it only Christians who seem to have difficulty with that claim, or is it just English people, or worse, both?

A group of high-powered Dominicans were arguing that *no* abortions could be allowed because *most* abortions would be wrong. They would not have argued in this way over any other ethical matter, for example, war. After three hours of the to and fro of debate, one of them exploded under the persistent questioning of two of those present. "All right, but in that case what is one going to do with all those little bitches who fuck around here, there, and everywhere?" So Jacques Pohier recounts in his book, *God in Fragments*. He comments that the group was using the life of a child and/or the life of a mother as a sexual deterrent. In the last resort the problem was posed by pleasure.

Because it is difficult to sustain pleasure without anarchy and hurt, we bring to it all manner of rules and prohibitions, and we try to narrow the purpose of sexuality. The extraordinarily vitriolic outbursts against those who have contracted the virus HIV III (which can lead to AIDS) is partly to be explained by the statement. "Serves them right for having had much more pleasure than I have ever done."

Moral condemnation seems to come into play much more easily where sex is concerned than in any other part of human life. The businessman who produces goods and makes money is not censured for the overwork that may have helped to cause

his ulcer or his coronary. The managers of mining companies
were not censured for allowing their miners to work in disease-
conducive circumstances: they were producers of coal, on
which the nation depended for its wealth. Of course certain
kinds of pleasure may have awful consequences, and pleasure
can mislead if these consequences are on a delayed fuse, but
this does not imply that pleasure is in itself and in all sexual
circumstances wrong. Sometimes sexual activity may need to
be safe from the risk of transmitting disease, and the best
conditions for relaxed pleasure may indeed be a relationship of
utter trust and commitment, thus providing a container for the
wildness and the passion that can tumble over into cruelty and
pain. But human lives would be more spiritual and Christian if
they knew more pleasurable sex and more erotically diffused
touch than seems usually to be the case.

Thomas Aquinas affirmed pleasure as one of the purposes of
sexuality. He argued that frameworks, including the virtue of
chastity, are devised for the maximizing of pleasure. He wrote
that continence is a sorry virtue because the will throttles the
passions. For the function of the will is not to be a tyrant, nor
that of the passions to be slaves. Continence merely gets in the
way of the purpose of the passions, which is pleasure. A
fifteenth century hymn exalts pleasure as one of the features of
life in heaven, a more fully embodied pleasure than anything
we know now:

> O how glorious and resplendent
> Fragile body shalt thou be
> When endued with so much beauty,
> Full of health, and strong, and free,
> Full of vigour, full of pleasure,
> That shall last eternally.

(Part of no. 401 in *English Hymnal*, translated by J. M. Neale)

The language of marriage includes both 'passion' and
'engagement', words that are also part of the language of holiness. To be saintly is to bring an intensity, an incandescence

almost, a depth of passion, to the ordinary and the everyday, so much so that a fierce gentleness is communicated in every action. A Carmelite monk, William McNamara (a contemplative celibate by vocation) writes that neither celibate nor married lovers are passionate enough: they are too lukewarm and nice. He would claim that passion is the gateway to God.

The psalmists, prophets, and mystics fume and weep and laugh with God: their spirituality engages their whole being and is full of energy. In the Old Testament it is not passion that is evil, but hardness of heart, callousness, insensitivity.

"For I saw with absolute certainty that our substance is in God, and moreover that he is in our sensuality too. The moment that the soul was made sensual, at that moment it was destined from all eternity to be the City of God. And he shall come to that city and never quit it." So Julian of Norwich wrote down the 55th of her *Revelations*, a fine example of embodied spirituality.

And here is an Italian poet, Guiseppe Caponsacchi, quoted by Alan Ecclestone in *Yes to God*:

> But she –
> The glory of life, the beauty of the world,
> The splendour of heaven . . . well, sirs, does no one move?
> Do I speak ambiguously? The glory, I say,
> And the beauty, I say, and the splendour, still say I,
> Who, a priest, trained to live my whole life long
> On beauty and splendour, solely at their source,
> God, have thus recognized my food in one . . .

That might almost be a comment on the psalmist (and I know the original is not clear) who felt that the Lord delighted not in any man's legs. I beg leave to disagree.

I suspect that this energy, courage, passionate activity and passivity, earthy and heavenly, are realities known much more deeply and wisely by woman than by man. Woman is more in touch with her sensuousness, with what can be touched and tasted, with sweat and blood, with the mysterious pulls of tides and waves, with stillness and with turbulence. (Andrea Dworkin puts it more eloquently in *Our Blood*.)

We know a lot about the domesticating of sex, with its wise continuities of families, hearth, and home. But there is this wildness to contend with as well, a yearning and a creating that seems to touch the fringes of the divine. Again it is a combination of passion and engagement that seems to spark that creativity.

When wild sexuality meets wild sexuality, it is all passion and explosion and horses' hooves cantering in the moonlight. By contrast, when domestic sexuality meets domestic, we have family contentment. More complex, when wild and domestic meet, the domestic may stop the wild from hurting others, giving some shape to the passion, and the wild may stop the domestic from being too tame. Where wounded sexuality meets domestic sexuality, there may be engagement, but no passion, and the couple may run a 'healing' script. Where wounded meets wounded, there may be only further hurt, unless both can be more aware of their needs and of what each is asking from the other. Where wounded meets wild, there will be disaster, for too much energy too soon is likely merely to deepen the wounds.

Churches and lawmakers have always had trouble with the wildness. If there is too much law, that which is angular, unconventional, creative, goes underground. If there is too little, anarchy ensues. Urban Holmes describes this dilemma in *The Sexuality of God*. Social and legal control over sexuality is notoriously superficial and cannot be otherwise. For we tend to be unaware – and we certainly do not like to be reminded – of the powerful energies so often out of touch with our conscious desires and choices. If we do contact the depths, and live from them, developing a new understanding of the power and complexity of our sexuality, we are bound to live to some degree out of step with the customs of the society we are part of. We are not safely predictable any more.

Yes, dark angels are troublesome, but there needs to be room in a mature society for the creative artists and prophets whose sexuality is often wild. I think it was John Osborne who said that a pram in the hallway is death to the creative artist. Such a person knows that a sexual encounter but once can be a symbolic act of communion, an effective sign of union and creativity that is about something beyond either or both of them, but does not take shape in the more usual ways of person-making, home-making, and the healing of wounds – all of which need the time-span of a commitment over many years.

It is fascinating to see how Teilhard de Chardin struggled with this insight in relation to his own vocation to celibacy. More than fifty years ago, when he was working in China, he wrote that he was becoming convinced that we should find another way of loving, that spiritual fruitfulness would become as valid a criterion for sexual relationships as the procreation of children, even the sole reason. He asked himself why sexual union should not be for the sake of the work of one or other of the couple, perhaps of work shared by both. He thought that such a purpose had been instinctively seized upon by creators of all kinds, who had not waited for moral approval. He mused, perhaps wryly, aware of the irony, that his own vocation to celibacy had been emotionally nourished by the work of those artists whose sexual lives, by the criteria of the times, had been irregular.

A French poet, Pierre Jean Jouvé, wrote in 1933 (translated by David Gascoyne and quoted in the magazine *Resurgence*, no. 124, 1987, p. 8): "We who are poets . . . must labour to bring forth, out of such base or precious substances as are derived from man's humble, beautiful erotic force, the 'bloody sweat' of sublimation." Here is a vocation to make the sexual sublime, not by becoming unearthly, but by sweat and passion, the passion that is both pleasure and pain. Indeed, as we spend our lives groaning and travailing in our creating (or, to use a phrase of Fr. Bill Kirkpatrick, our co-creating), a purely relaxed pleasure may be a rare luxury.

The wildness, then, is risky, too near to chaos for the comfort of the bureaucrats. I read in the community newspaper in Earl's Court in London that the local council had been using pesticides to tidy Brompton Cemetery. A local resident had complained that, as a result, there were fewer species of animals and plants and birds than had been observable a few years previously. The writer was arguing for a little wildlife conservation in the middle of the city. Few of the graves in the older part of the cemetery are now cared for, and even in the rest there is no more room for new graves. But it seems that we prefer the tidy edge, knowing exactly where grave ends and path begins. We prefer the neatly kept gardens of remembrance with regimented rosebeds rather than graveyards that are occasionally and mildly pruned. Are we afraid of reminders of the wilderness that we cannot control, of death too that we cannot control? The nature we wish to tame, rather than contemplate and co-operate with, is, in its insects and grasses, tougher than we are. Maybe too the authorities dislike the unconventional sexual activity that is reputed to occur in the bushes, the activity of those who can find no other privacy than the rampant undergrowth obscuring the reminders of our mortality . . .

9
Listening to woman-sexuality

In the process of the maturing of our sexuality, through pleasure, passion, and the healing of wounds, we can call on two helpers, two languages, that of woman-sexuality and that of touch. I have mentioned both already, and wish simply to highlight them a little more. Both languages have been around for a long time, but both are being heard in new ways and more insistently, even in the sacristy and the officers' mess.

I do not have the authority to write much about woman-sexuality, and what little I have comes from the women who have trusted me with their stories. In the listening I certainly become aware of what woman-sexuality is not.

It is not the wildness of man-sexuality on the loose, that dominates and uses the power of force to get its own way.

It is not the fury of woman, usually hidden under a cloak of conditioned compliance with her 'man', devaluing her own worth and her own sexuality.

It is not a sexuality that is all sweetness and light, for it does have its own strength and power. (Some *men* have in fact always been suspicious of the myth of the weaker sex: should we not be seeking to express our mutual need of two complementary kinds of strength, each redeeming the other from domination or manipulation?)

It is not a sexuality that is split, split into three parts: the mother and virgin who is the guardian of home and family; the servant who is the property of her husband; the witch who is carnal and full of evil passion. Such interpretations have come from men.

Woman is not defective male. The thinking of Aristotle still distorts us. He claimed that mother-mater-matter supplies the raw material of a new human being, the father providing the soul. To be female is to be rounded and sloppy, not able to create form out of matter. If the male masters the female and

40

imposes his form on matter, then there will be born a formed and angular son, not a plump and shapeless daughter. So the female is thought to be a 'misbegotten' and 'defective' male. Such a quaint biological understanding persisted a long time, affecting far more than just biology. Even early modern science pictured spermatozoa as containers with homunculi inside, miniature fully formed males.

No longer are women content to have their sexuality defined and controlled by men. New thinking is coming out of woman-awareness and woman-power, some of it on the loose, as dangerous in its way as man-sexuality on the loose, but the exploration is needed if there is to be a more mature and profound living of our human sexuality, both as men and as women, and as the two relating to each other.

I have already mentioned Andrea Dworkin. Morley Callaghan, in her novel, *They Shall Inherit the Earth*, describes one of her characters, Anna, in words like 'fulness' and 'wholeness'. You immediately see before you a woman and not a man, a human being who can just be, rather like a piece of pottery on a table that is simply there in its own completeness, claiming its space in quiet strength. We use the phrase, 'to possess one's own soul', to describe a state of being fully present and alive; it is rarer in men, and it is the very opposite of pride and possessiveness.

Again Rilke is amazingly prophetic of the new contribution woman is making to the living out of human sexuality. In Letter 7 you sense he is describing the same kind of human being that Morley Callaghan does. He sees a fruitfulness and confidence of being in a woman that is missing in a man in his presumption and hastiness. She is *human* in her own right, not merely the opposite of man, even though she has probably been taught to think she needed her 'other half' in order to be herself. But she can be a rounded and complete person as *herself*.

So human sexual loving relationships will, hopes Rilke, become those of one human being to another, not of man to woman as now experienced. He sees such a relationship as considerate and fulfilling, gentle and clear, 'two solitudes' who protect each other's uniqueness, and who know the appropriate space between them, and how and when it is right to touch and greet.

Such insight begins to take us beyond the wild and the domestic and the wounded, into a much wiser sexuality, characterized not least by a diffused, whole-body eroticism. There will be more of that in Chapter 11. First there are some questions to be brought together about touch that in the answering will also point us in that direction.

10

Learning the language of touch

It makes an interesting exercise in self-examination to ask some questions about exactly what is going on in ourselves and in others at moments of physical touch. It is rare to find such questions, let alone the answers, in the literature of faith. But here are some. They are deeply spiritual questions.

What is there in my touching that should bring forth from me either gratitude or penitence?

What does a particular touch mean in the context of the rest of that particular relationship?

Is a particular touch a profound symbol of relationship and communion, or is it merely a formal sign, like a perfunctory handshake?

To become aware of such questions as and when we touch and are touched is to begin to grow in a new way spiritually.

Further, what is there of pleasure in my touching? Without it, an encounter of flesh-bodies can hardly be an act of love. And a further question immediately presses. Will ardent touch and passion give pleasure to this person now, or will it give pain because it is too powerfully energetic? At the other extreme, a tender, almost feather-like touch, affectionate, even playful, while giving comfort and delight to one, may give pain to another, for whom it is too indefinite in its quality, not secure and firm enough to allow tense muscles to relax, to allow trust to deepen. An exploration of massage could well be included in courses of marriage preparation!

Much of our difficulty stems from fear. Mellors, the game-keeper in D.H. Lawrence's *Lady Chatterley's Lover*, complains of our fear of touch, a fear that leaves us half-dead. For Lawrence, sex is the closest and most tender touch, the most delicate of encounters. He sees it as the crying need of the English! But many men react to such tenderness as though they are afraid that it will unman them, and they dismiss it as effete and 'wet'.

43

We are also afraid that touch will be violent, violating, in some way we cannot always grasp, inappropriately intrusive. Perhaps you were once told in an outburst of anger which took you by surprise and which you could not understand. ''Don't touch yourself there.'' Perhaps the only way in which touch was allowed with another of your own sex – if you were a boy – was in the rough and tumble of a fight. Perhaps you were taken advantage of sexually in childhood, even if only mildly, and you have repressed the memory, and this has made you wary. A trustworthy and healing touch can indeed be our crying need.

I think we also need to recognize that the touch of healer and priest, of nurse and masseur, takes up the energy of the sexual and uses it. Of course this is not a focussed, genital touch, but I am not sure that the erotic is totally absent. After all, if sexual energy is about the desire to be united with others (and within oneself and with God), and about the desire to create (both a new being and a new sense of being), then it has its place in the diffused touching that helps another person become more whole.

There is a sensitive passage in James Baldwin's novel, *Another Country*, in which Vivaldo is telling Eric about the last time he had been with Rufus, whose death he is mourning. He remembers that he had not wanted to leave Rufus alone that particular night, and had sensed that he was being asked to hold him close. He had known that genital sex was not being asked for, though it might have happened. But if so, it would have been incidental to the need for comfort and healing. Fear had held Vivaldo back – would his touch have been misinterpreted? And the fear had held at bay the love in his heart. Now he wonders if his reaching out across the mere quarter of an inch that had separated them on the bed would have saved Rufus from despair. Of course, he would never know . . .

We have to ask ourselves seriously whether our sins of omission might include those occasions when we have lacked courage, and in our fear failed to reach out and touch another.

Of course such touch is not automatically clear and truthful at a time when the boundaries of relationships are not as clear as once they were. Jack Burton, in his humorous and frank diary, *Transport of Delight*, has wrestled with the exhilaration and complexity of loving others when fully aware of the flow of sexual energy. Yes, our lives and the lives of our partners and families can be enriched by all manner of other relationships which have their spring, however unacknowledged, in sexual attraction and energy. But no wonder the maps have warned, 'Here be dragons'. What kind of touch can keep such relationships in love and truth? Looks and smiles? Sparkling eyes? Touch of hands? of arms? of shoulders? of hair? of lips? What intimacy, what variety, what pleasure? Is it wisdom or fear that lies behind the old boundary-mark that said, 'All for one and none for anyone else'? How do we respond to the possibilities of passionate touch, of tender touch, of sexually aware touch, in circumstances where one person's boundary may be different from the other's?

I suspect that many potentially rich relationships founder because each of the two people involved is reacting differently to the impinging of one flesh-body on another, and neither is able to articulate what the difference is. A comforting closeness for one may be almost suffocation for another. What distance and what closeness are appropriate? Each relationship is different. How, by our touch and lack of touch, by a generous movement towards another and by a genuine restraint, do we actually express what we feel about protection, welcome, retreat, expulsion? How much does one feel hard-pressed by the other, how much freed by the other?

Much of our inheritance of faith and culture suggests that there should be clear limits to our touching. Israel of old always had enemies and untouchables. The wall, inner and outer, that surrounded them, was a high one. Notions of pollution held that people would be a danger to others if they crossed certain boundaries. Notions of holiness suggested that the sacred must be protected, and that the ones who transgressed taboos must be excluded. But what if flesh-body itself is holy ground? Must not any No to another person always be with the intention of reaching a more profound and richer Yes? If there is a No to genital sexual expression on moral or health grounds, what kind of touch might express a deeper Yes to the other?

We find any steps beyond the conventions of our upbringing risky and at least a little frightening. To go beyond our own kin and our own kind? We prefer the safety of the known, and sense that a close encounter with the unknown will change us unpredictably. So we build our fear into systems of belief about the purity of the race. We believe we are protecting ourselves from disturbance. There must be no mixing of blood.

Certainly it is risky to mix, but there is no future life and little present love without risk. Exchange of body fluids has always contained a hint of danger. Where there is new life and new love, deadly disease and death have never been distant. But those who live on the slopes of volcanoes know that they till some of the world's richest soil. Prudence may be one thing; avoidance of disturbance is another. You cannot be creative and totally safe at the same time.

Can we then get beyond the instant reaction of categorizing people when we ask ourselves whom we should like to touch? Can we recognize our skin not so much as the boundary that separates us from others as the porous point of contact where in kiss or sweat we first mingle the flow of fluids and of flesh?

Such questions as these are frightening to those who are schizoid – and that is a word that describes most people in our culture. It is easier to escape from the challenge of intimacy – into words, into computers, into formality of contact with others. And words in our culture have lost much of their passion and earthiness: they have become as mechanical as our relating. They have become devalued through propaganda and technology. They do not easily mediate the holy, cannot often be sacramental, cannot without difficulty resonate with a whisper of the beyond. The most that talk about touch can do is to give encouragement to learn its language, not to be afraid of starting a new ABC, however foolish we may feel, to make an act of faith that the language of flesh-body is trustworthy. The body does not lie. Flesh-body can indeed be the place of truth, and can be the best means of grace.

When we have begun to come home to ourselves in this way, then we may again be attuned to the finer wavelengths of words. And the poet, testing that faith and experiencing that grace, catching in strange places a scent of the hope of glory, may find the occasional words that are no longer an escape, but genuinely mark the path for others.

II

Tuning more finely

As we explore our sexuality, we begin to discern its various rhythms – the ardent and the tender; the enlivening and the quietening; the passionate and the gentle; the exciting and the relaxing; the letting go and the letting be; the range of the language of touch and its finer tuning. So we begin to learn what it is like to diffuse our sexuality, to let sensation spread throughout the entire flesh-body, head, heart, guts, loins. Perhaps the next stage in description would be to talk of mystical union – with the inner self, with the other, with God – an experience which, however refined, is still an experience of the living organism.

Let me re-cap, using the four Greek words that have been associated with sexuality and love. First is 'epithymia' or 'libido': this is raw desire, raw sex. Sensation is sought, and release of tension. It is self-centred. The impulse is that of need. It easily results in a closing-in on flesh-body alone. There is no caring: the other is perceived as object or thing. 'Eros' implies at least a desire for union, for communion with another, for creativity. 'Libido' and 'eros' together point to the desired, yearned for lover, and for a passionate sexual relationship. Add to these 'philia', the quality of affection and friendship, and we have the desired, yearned for friend, and for a sexual relationship that is full of compassion and tenderness. Lastly there is 'agape', with its quality of goodwill, care, and courtesy, its willingness to stop at nothing to enable the good of the beloved. This releases 'libido', 'eros', and 'philia' from any tendency towards self-centredness and possessiveness. It protects the solitude of the other, letting be, withdrawing for a time when need be, leaving a space between.

When all these four together are active in a relationship, the one person is able to say to the other: "I know that your sexuality is not on the loose and that you will be here for me

48

tomorrow; I know that you are lustily passionate; I know that you do not always have to be genital, and that you are not afraid to be tender; I know that you are not trying to possess me."

If there is only 'libido', the result is dispersed sex: there is hardly any flesh-body in it. 'Eros' adds the flesh-body, and sexual activity becomes focussed. 'Philia' enables a restraint of passion, but the whole of flesh-body can still communicate a sexual energy, albeit diffused. With 'agape' the flesh-body can become – words begin to fail – translucent, aglow, trans-figured, paradoxically dependent on a quality of loving that does not need physically to touch but can flourish even over the distances of years and miles. Perhaps the 'soul-body' is beginning to shine through – but more of that in the next chapter.

For the moment, let me stay with the thought of a diffused sexuality. How might we widen and deepen our experience of it? It is partly a matter of being convinced of values not often known in a culture that is too focussed on genital sex. Might it not be, however, that diffused sexual activity could be as satisfying as the genital, so long as there is contact, touch, warmth? Both parties may be affected deeply. Love is still being made. The sexual energy, however, has become more like the hum of a dynamo than the crackle of a fire.

Does 'sleeping together' necessarily imply genital sex? It takes quite a deep trust to fall asleep in the arms of another, of either gender, the touching now being a quietening rather than an arousing. In the *Teaching of Joseph Smith*, the founder of the Mormons, we read: "When we lie down together, we contem-plate how we may rise in the morning: and it is pleasing for friends to lie down together, locked in the arms of love, to sleep and awake in each other's embrace and renew their conver-sation." Is that breathtakingly naive, or wisdom?

A diffused sexuality can be approached by the Way of Contradictions, with its restraint of touch needed to treat the wounds with care, and it can be reached by the Way of

Affirmations, the point where focussed sexuality yields nothing creative any more for the two people concerned (or where, for one reason or another, it is no longer possible).

A transformation begins to take place: it is often imperceptible, like a deep underground river, hardly perceived by the sensations of flesh-body, yet located there nonetheless. A subtle vibration is set in motion by the quality of loving and the rhythms of loving, through times of desert and of oases; through darkness and storm, and through moments of the flashing of monstrance and the steadiness of domestic lamps. A glow, a radiance, a harmony begins to shine through. The divine is interpenetrating the human. "I share in the light," said St. Symeon the Theologian. "I participate in the glory, and my face shines like my Beloved's, and all my members become bearers of light." (*Hymns of Divine Love*, no. 16.)

The sexual has so often been described in religious literature as a helpful way of making comparisons with the divine, the divine which is thought to be something wholly different from and other than the sexual. Here I am suggesting that the sexual is a *parable* of the divine, a sample of the divine, a 'knowing' of God: it is not the fulness of eternity, but is at least a foretaste of it.

In his fourth letter, Rilke suggests yet another dimension. Our creativity, in sex and work, connects with that of every living being and with our own ancestors. Artists may need the protection of solitude if the creative process is to flow, but they are never solitary in the sense of being isolated from life. Whether this 'making the new' occurs in a brief wild moment of delight, or with a more sustained and gentle flow of 'inspiration', it is being continually affirmed by everything and everyone around us. Each creative act can be full of an awareness of millions of such acts that have occurred through the generations. The sensations may be diffuse, and the birthing may be hard and long, within the being of the artist, but any creative activity belongs to our sexuality, and is to be recognized and enjoyed as such.

An afterthought – or is it a forethought, pushing out in advance of our experience? Might it be conceiveable that celibate people (sexually alive, of course, but not expressing that sexuality genitally in a committed relationship) could learn the language of touch in such a way as to experience such subtle vibrations of pleasure so intensely that orgasm as we know it would become an irrelevance? By concentrating on when orgasms are allowable, in a historical atmosphere of hostility to the flesh, we may have missed a crucial insight: we are called to let our sexuality be a means of creating pleasure and love among us: if that happened more readily in a diffused way, then we might even reach the point of being content to leave orgasms to the occasions when procreation is desired. That is to make a point in an extreme fashion, pleasing neither conservative nor liberal. Certainly we are a long way from understanding the call to celibacy as a call to celebrate sexuality in a profoundly physical and fleshly way that might be even more enjoyable and delightful than the current statistical norm. But is the eunuch, reproductively infertile (whether by illness or genetic inheritance or by deliberate choice of restraint), but not impotent, not physically castrated, the one who is challenged to use sexuality in a spiritually fertile way through all manner of touch, ninety-nine point nine percent beyond our imagining?

12

Being transfigured

THROUGH our sexuality we are being lured by the Divine Lover into eternal life, resurrection life, supra-fleshly life. As it is now, flesh-body participates in the process of learning to become open to transfiguration. We do this through experiencing our sexuality coming into contact, through other human beings, with the drawing power of an awesome and insistent Presence of Love, the Holy Spirit, the invisible Go-Between God continually re-orientating us through ways of affirmation and contradiction. Here is the activity of God Incognito, God in prepositions as it were, a Presence within us, among, between, behind, before us.

So the 'soul-body' is being formed, as yet only fitfully, a form of being known in moments of flesh-body meeting, of radiance, ecstasy, healing, and gentleness, of accurate touch of truth and love. Such are the times when the seeds of a resurrection-body are nurtured, seeds that one day will be freed to grow unrestricted by space or time. And that nurturing may still happen through the most painful of contradictions in this life, even if the seed is merely being protected in the dark earth, or lying on a desert floor waiting for years for a single shower of rain to bring it to life. In any case passion itself is also being more finely tuned until – *pace* Michelangelo – the reach of a finger will be enough to spark a universe. And it is the sexual energies that will have triggered this more subtle 'stuff' – waves, vibrations, particles – of soul-body, of resurrection-body. Others have called it a 'hatching of the heart'.

St. Isaac the Syrian wrote of these marks of the loving heart, these characteristics of soul-body life: it is a heart that burns with love for the whole creation, men and women, birds and beasts, for the demons, for all creatures, a love that radiates fleshly warmth, a love that is an immense compassion, suffering in solidarity, a love that expresses itself in the details of material and bodily care. Whatever is beyond death is that *and more*, not an existence ethereal and ghostly.

So a person's Truest Self in recognizable form is not flesh-body, but stuff triggered into being by the Spirit of God in and through flesh-body life, inseparable from it, and very much needing it, indeed unable to be brought into being without it – soul-body, resurrection body, spiritual body. Each of these words is important: *soul*-body because it is a body as yet mostly hidden (rather than because souls might be thought to have no substance); *spiritual*-body because it is a reality known but not fully experienced in this life; *resurrection*-body because it is Jesus who pioneered the way through the godly-bodily quality of his presence and life among us, and because the forming of this new body, as it was with Jesus, is the work of *God* (it is *not* automatic survival, rather an incorporation into Christ's Resurrection, Christ, who, embodied still, is part and parcel of the dynamic life of God in which we begin to share, becoming 'partakers of the divine nature' – 2 Peter 1.4); lastly, all these phrases contain the word *body* because we are talking about this world's stuff transformed, not an *entirely* different world of so-called spirits. The context too is vast: the destiny embraces more than individuals, for, as Gregory of Nyssa said, the whole of nature must be raised from the dead. So this new reality is not less than flesh, rather much more than flesh. The old language of the *resurrection of the flesh* is largely misleading, since it does not mean the resuscitation of corpses, but it does point to the abiding reality of recognition, communion, creativity, union, all of which we know now *through the flesh*. Eternal life, then, is super-flesh-body life, or supra-flesh-body life. E. L. Mascall reminds us in *The Christian Universe* that our enjoyment of God the other side of the grave will be more ecstatic and passionate than anything we have known in this life.

When we remember in prayer those who have died before us, perhaps part of the prayer is a request to them that they more richly make love than they ever did on earth, in such a way that their love overflows to our benefit. Is not their – and our – making love, in our different forms of being, what is meant by our being partners with God in creating?

There is of course a catch. I gather it has been said that after the age of 40 we are responsible for our faces, and by the age of 50 we have the faces we deserve. Through the flesh-body, and particularly through our faces, we show something of the truth of ourselves. We may do much to disguise it (with 'cosmetics' we create our own artificial 'cosmos' which we show to the world), but hidden truth will come to light, and the observant will see in unlikely moments truths about ourselves that we usually take good care to cover up. It makes you wonder just what the expressions on our faces will be like when we cannot disguise the truth any longer. For as well as a process of transfiguration, which is open to us if we are open to the Spirit of God at work in and through our flesh-body selves, there is also a process of disfiguration with which we have to struggle. There is the battering that life gives us anyway, together with the more subtle changes that occur when we allow our compass to drift or when we deliberately set it away from God. At the very least, the faces of our soul-body selves will bear scars.

But let not that truth distract us too much from affirming the value of flesh-body life, nor the worth of each human being as unique and more than mammal. Only then can we face the truth that there is no ultimate value to be placed on the flesh-body (it cannot of itself inherit the Commonwealth of God) because there is something greater in store. Death is real, but it is not the end, and it need not be denied. In fact, the more at home we are as flesh-bodies the less do we need to fear death. I suspect that women know more of this than men, and on the whole are less afraid. Death is beyond the control that men like to exercise: they do not like to reckon with the unpredictable. Women already know drastic flesh-body change through menstruation and pregnancy, and so have intimations of the greatest change of all.

We may the more delight in flesh-body the more we learn not to fear death: and we may hope in soul-body and thus the more easily bear with earthly limitations. In the hymn for Pentecost, *Come down, O Love divine*, I know that the word 'earthly' means 'worldly' in the prayer that 'earthly passions' may 'turn to dust and ashes' in the Spirit's 'consuming': I wonder if it might be a more Christian prayer that they may turn to gold and silver in the Spirit's heat refining.

NB. I have been using the word 'body' in much the same way as John A. T. Robinson used it in his book *The Body*. He delves deeply into the meaning of the Greek word 'soma', the word in the New Testament somewhat unsatisfactorily translated 'body', and more accurately meaning the whole personality and living organism, both in ourselves and in relationship to others. Our 'bodiliness' is caught up in the process of our redemption: we are delivered from the 'soma' of sin and death through the 'soma' of Christ on the Cross; we are incorporated into Christ's 'soma' the Church and, as a community, are sustained by his 'soma' in the Eucharist. In our 'soma' the life of Christ is shown, and we are destined in the resurrection of this 'soma' to share in the likeness of Christ's glorious 'soma'.

13
Becoming pain-bearers

JAMES NELSON reminds us that we are all sexually deformed, by one or other of a depressing list of feelings and experiences: by guilt, by shame, by fear, by dualistic attitudes and actions, by physical and emotional abuse, by homophobia, by silence. We sometimes think we live in enlightened times, but are they all that enlightened?

Perhaps all this talk of pleasure and passion and tenderness and supra-flesh-bodies serves but to re-open an old and painful wound.

Perhaps you can feel any touch as nothing more than a sensation of the skin, cold and lifeless, sealed off from warmth and feeling.

Perhaps sexuality has always meant torment and humiliation, more like a life sentence than a means of grace.

Perhaps sex is simply awful and inescapable. Husbands must have their rights, and Friday night is duty night. For many women that is no laugh.

Perhaps sex is yearned for but impossible in the way you desire: you may be physically disabled, or carry a potentially lethal virus.

Perhaps you simply have to accept a wound to the emotions that, lived with, may make you creative but will often leave you feeling lonely and exhausted.

In a radio interview, the composer Sir Michael Tippett said: "I also understood that there was a deep wound. I didn't in the end want to blame anybody for it, or the society or myself. I didn't quite understand what the wound was. I don't to this day . . . Well, there it was, you had to live with it. I never was driven, because of my temperament or whatever, never after the self-analysis was there any special pleading of any kind. I once said to myself I shall never have a shoulder to cry on, I didn't want one." (*The Listener*, 14.viii.87)

Perhaps a quiet but desperate misery drowns all other sounds within you, layer after layer of unhappiness. Perhaps the only thing to do is to bear it in your heart, and listen for another voice deeper still, another sound not easily caught, an occasional snatch on the wind. But the two sounds together might be extended into a duet more beautiful than either voice alone could possibly be. Afterwards the realization may dawn that the note of misery has become part of a tune of glory.

It is hard to live with a wound, to know the kind of pain that is never entirely absent, to have hoped for healing but to have had that hope dashed. It has not happened, and now it is impossible. The wound lies too deep in the groin: maybe it was inflicted unknowingly, at the time of that earliest of our confinements. Perhaps we can all sense something of Auden's remark that our flesh is really at home only when its terrors come.

It is the loneliness that most find the hardest reality to bear, though it can be turned sometimes into prayer or art. What of the widow in the high-rise flat who is housebound and has few callers? Can she meet the challenge to move from a closed-in loneliness to a solitude full of others, loved in prayerful holding to the Presence of God? Hers will be no obviously chosen vocation of contemplation, but she might dare to look with loving eyes on her own wound and the world's wound, and offer it all to the Greater Love.

The loneliness may turn to the solitude of the artist, again an unclear mix of the necessary and the chosen. There will be a tussle with the art, in love and hate, attraction and repulsion. Tippett found that no one-to-one relationship would work because "I was locked in this everlasting obsessive bloody music." (*op.cit.*)

This is indeed the way of deepest contradictions, which takes you through everything that, as flesh-body, you would rebel against. But the inescapable, once deeply accepted, freely embraced, can become destiny, and even give a rare joy, its colours dark but rich. It is a way that the artist has charted best. It involves space, solitude, silence, a living in 'nada', which is Spanish for 'nothing'. It involves a waiting, a darkness, and a painful birthing.

Again, Rilke is my guide. He tells the young poet that he must wait in a solitude that is so large and so protected that there is no opportunity for escape. There are bound to be times when any human contact, however trivial and unworthy, would feel better than the endurance imposed on him. But the artist, to produce anything that is more than banal, must be able to go deep within and remain there for at least hours at a time. Rilke compares this with growing pains, the growth actually happening when the feelings are most discordant, like the struggle of the emerging adolescent or of spring after winter.

It is necessary to endure the darkness. All gestation takes place in the dark. There has to be a time of letting the inexpressible remain inexpressible, deep in the dark unconscious, and neither grasp prematurely at understanding nor shape what may be emerging while its outline is still unclear. This demands great humility and patience. It may be as painful as a dancer who has but a tiny cell in which to dance. No movement can be complete: there is not enough room for the sequence of steps or the swinging of arms. Perhaps only his lips can shape the dance, perhaps his battered fingers have to trace the lines on the walls of the cell.

If that is true for a Rilke, for a poet or an artist, it is also true for the counsellor, who has to negotiate the dark with the suffering person who has come to tell his story; she has to wait for a new birth from within the silence and the space, a birth over which she has no control. And the very space that the counsellor has learned to inhabit as a result of facing her own wound and loneliness, is itself a gift that helps that process to become fruitful. How many of us give the other person room to breathe, to be open? Yet it is a quality needed in every close relationship, not only a counselling one.

Vast distances always separate us because of our uniqueness as individuals. Sexual desire may bring us face to face, but this can be too close at times. If we can accept the space between, then we can grow side by side. We have to learn to love that space. Only then will we see each other as we truly are. We may then be surprised how beautiful the other looks against the backcloth of the sky.

Space, silence, solitude, waiting, darkness, gestation, birth: is not this the experience of each of us coming to be in the womb? Is it not also the Virginity of the God-Bearer? Is it not a virginity that is openness, rather than the negative definition of that word, 'no sex yet'? For we are talking of a welcome to someone other into that space, bearing with the other, accepting the temporary helplessness of the other, so that the other may be born in God. This seems to be a quality of being known by all women, even the child-bearers, for whom most of the time over the years the womb is empty. Is this both pain and opportunity?

This understanding of virginity points to a quality of life that can survive and flourish even if the flesh is vulnerable and wounded, even if a human being has been physically bloodied and blighted, even if a woman is barren. Counsellors seek to be channels of a healing river that can wash such blood from off the sand. As a result, there may be a deeper acceptance by the other both of the wounds and of the need to remain open to others. The counsellor's own emptiness is put at the service of others. And is it not simply this humble, alert, open quality of presence that redeems, the wounded physician who heals? The one with the limp sets the bones of others straight. We may each of us know a measure of healing, but it often seems as if that is so only that we might be able to bear the pains of others. Saving them, we cannot save ourselves. In a way, the better the counsellor is at her job, the better the human being is at his living, the more is the pain that can be transformed, and the more exhausted we shall be from the fray. The sword will be endlessly piercing our hearts. Yet in the very centre of our being which is perpetual openness, which is pain-bearing, in that very place others may find a vast expanse of solitude in which they can learn to be at home and breathe quite freely. The ground between shimmers, it becomes holy ground, a burning bush of presence, a mountaintop of transfiguration, an empty tomb, a place of revelation, a sign of glory.

It is a high vocation to be a pain-bearer, yet common to all humanity. We are challenged to respond to a call of a new creation whose seeds lie in the contradictions of the flesh, a call that lures us by its faint but increasingly irresistible invitation, the whisper of a thunder on a distant shore. It is Eliot's intolerable sheet of flame whose unfamiliar name is Love.

This is *not* to say that we have finally discovered the only true path to holiness, having left sexuality far behind, that this is what we have been waiting for, this is *real* spirituality. No, this is not a superior vocation, it is a dimension of a universal human vocation, but one that some find themselves living sooner or more intensely than most people do. They find that for them the most deeply creative thing happens in the place of sexual solitude. It may simply be that this is what God is up to in them, transforming their particular piece of intractable human clay to glory, however disorientating and puzzling the process often turns out to be.

"Experience of profound change, where accepted patterns are distorted rather than reinforced, may lead to a state of disorientation and normlessness, and explanations sought in the stored learning of the past do not satisfy in situations where what was is no longer. But consent must be given, for partial meanings will not satisfy. All that is certain is uncertainty, and stability is as transient as the balance of a spinning top: occasional familiar landmarks loom out of the mist and dissolve like phantoms. The reorientation involves looking at patterns of light and shade and colour in reflections in a stream without recognizing what is being reflected. Defences keep trying to stop the reorientation: fatigue and failure are common. Even while consent is given, a rearguard action is being fought to preserve the old securities. But the other dimension continues to press, and longing and desire focusses on the Beyond. And you have to wait for the meaning to come." (Anon. *Reflections in a Moving Stream.* 1982)

At such a time of change, to go back is to experience Love as Wrath, no longer life-giving. Of course we do go back, or at least we try, snarling our tyres in those metal prongs that lie down only if we are travelling in the right direction. And yes, our resistances and defences need to be respected: it is disastrous to try and dismantle them all at once. All in all it will be an 'apocalyptic' time, a time of tribulation. (The word 'tribulation' in the original Greek refers to the squeezing of olives or grapes in the press.) When that experience is undergone by countless individuals, so that it becomes a mark of the time in which they live, then we can truly talk of an end-time, an apocalypse of a whole civilization. For peoples as well as for individuals, what was once good may no longer be so; the armour of dinosaurs is no longer protective of life. Something better is afoot, even if obscure and less obviously fulfilling.

But when you are living, somewhere, somehow, from the depths, from a deeper place than ever before, and you continue to act in a way that was once creative but is now out of balance, when you are at the limits of the framework of your life, at the edges of the known, there is bound to be a grating and a snarling: it is Love coming to you with the face of Wrath. For example, a sexual relationship may have enabled two people to grow in love and freedom, but they may have reached the point where the directly sexual can give no more: the sexual now serves only to make them aware of boundaries that cannot be crossed that way, and a certain distancing is needed between them. Or a person may have begun to realize the limitations of a pattern of dispersed sexual experience, and be faced with the risk of a deep sexual love and commitment for the first time. It is painful to go through such a time of change, and at the same time to be aware of others continuing, seemingly contentedly and creatively, within what you now perceive only at the limits – a rich domesticity maybe, or a fiery passion, or even a dedicated solitude. But for all of us, sooner or later, and certainly by the time of our dying, limits, inherent in all earthly experience and relationships, will be increasingly sensed as a pressure to seek another 'world', another place from which to live more completely. And that will be a lonely time, often of agony, through a narrow gate, before we reach the new wide open spaces beyond. The way involves real loss, a sacrifice, a giving up of something we have valued – or, worse, something that we wanted and needed and never had. But we will be taking the goodness of those needs and desires with us along with the loss, and through the apparent complete negating, be given a deeper and wider goodness that includes and transcends even the best of what we have known or desired.

Plods through the wilderness are no tourist tasting of the desert: they have been reputed to last forty years – that is Hebrew code for a tiresomely long time. You cannot put down roots in any known geographical or inner place. You can but reach out for your new identity into the future, into the "I Shall Be Who I Shall Be" who has a delight in appearing in wildernesses and on frontiers (as he did to Jacob in his dreams), the One who is absolutely committed to loving creativity whatever the cost, suffering passionately to transform all the negativities and contradictions of our sexuality through the spaces, the pain, the distances, the impossibilities of the flesh.

God knows (or perhaps doesn't) what is happening as the old individual, the old ego, the old civilization crumbles and we cannot discern the shape of the new. All that we can trust is the conviction that there is no limit to the ability of divine love to sustain and transform the creation through these periods of disintegration. It is always thus in apocalyptic times: times of sifting, of disorientation, of krisis, of faint hopes of God.

In his book, *If Not Now, When?*, Primo Levi writes of a band of Russian Jewish partisans behind enemy lines in the forests and marshes of Eastern Europe at the end of the Second World

War. They invent a way of keeping a fire going while dispersing the smoke through a constructed mesh of branches, so as to escape the notice of planes flying overhead. When they make contact with another camp, the narrator notices the same construction there. He comments that certain discoveries happen, apparently independently, when the time is ripe, because circumstances are such that there is only one solution to the problem.

I am trying to discern as clearly as I can, having in mind von Hügel's dictum about the two clarities. If what I am writing is eccentric and nonsense, it will deservedly soon be forgotten: few people will read it anyway. But if it is at all prophetic, it will be found not be be unique to the writer, but will resonate in the inner being of at least some of those who read, and it will be found in retrospect to tune in with what others have been more adequately expressing at about the same time. Indeed, this whole book feels like an exploration of questions, a looking into a moving stream and finding the reflections confusing. I simply know that it is important to keep on looking.

In Primo Levi's book, the leader of the partisan band, Mendel, meets the captain of a regular Russian army unit. The captain admits that he envies them because they have written a new story. They have taken charge of their destiny, and what they have learned in the forest and marshes he is convinced must not be lost. He is adamant that the lesson can survive only in people who have learned the new thing: it will be frozen again if it is simply recorded in a book. The narrator adds that Mendel felt as if he had been seized by an eagle and carried into the sky. Yes, to *have* to pioneer other ways of loving may similarly claw at the very being of those who have no choice but to embrace their destiny either with despair or with delight. It feels a lonely task, but if dilemmas have a solution, they will be found more or less at the same time by many others, simply because old answers no longer satisfy, and the problem, complex as it is in the unravelling, has but one solution.

It is the *experience* of thousands that really counts: the writer can but reflect that experience through his own hunches and imagination. If what he writes is true, it is important that it survives in more than a book. And it keeps the writer in his place to reflect that the founder of Christianity is never recorded as writing anything save a few marks with a stick in the sand.

None of this is to deny the lessons that can be learned, and seem so rarely to have been tackled in religious circles, about the ways of affirmation of our sexuality. Nor is it to deny that the risks of loving may lead the person who has found some healing space in the depths of solitude to a new kind of creativity through a sexual relationship. But it is, for example, to believe that those working through the sufferings caused by AIDS, with all the woundedness and wildness and contradictions associated with this disease, are also the pioneers through suffering of a new way of loving, new ways of 'being in touch' because of being 'out of touch' with the old, and because none of us can bear isolation. Even the hermit's aloneness must be warmed by Love into an in-touchness, however painful, with flesh-body, or it will be detached from the corporate body of humankind on whose behalf she has embraced her solitude.

If we share, even fitfully and falteringly, in such a vocation of bearing the pain of an end time and beginning time, we may be helping to prepare a new birth of God, and so hasten the fulfilment of the purposes of Love, the true 'end' of the world, and the completion of the Divine Commonweal.

Responding to a conference

WORDS are slippery and dangerous. Some of you have affirmed my words by saying that they have clarified and encouraged. Others have said that they have felt seduced and humiliated. I certainly know – or at least partly know – that there are confusions among the galaxy of ideas, there is theological untidiness, there are no doubt discrepancies between the words and the speaker, whose unresolved pathology will have caused some distortion.

The wavelengths emitted by a speaker will have at least four patterns: that of the words of the public persona, that of the counsellor who has tried to listen to the stories of others, that of an ordinary human being in social and personal relationships, and that of an extra-ordinary human being on a unique journey, with all its stumblings and vulnerabilities, as well as its understandings and perceptions, hard and finely wrought. I have sought clarity, but I can hardly hope to have avoided some confusion.

Confusion is made visible in the chapel of this Pastoral Centre. We have ignored the logic of its architecture by not focussing our attention eastwards, where the patterns of the tracery of the window, whether by accident or design I do not know, show us phallus and vagina together, man and woman in harmony. Perhaps we have turned our backs because we are now painfully aware of the contrast between that calm statement in stone and our own confusions about sexuality and faith. We have also ignored the west door, and so missed the opportunity of entering and leaving the chapel beneath the rose window, a mandala of completion, with its rays of sun beaming out from the Dove-Spirit in the centre. It is as if we find these symbols too confident, too assured. In our perplexity we do not know which way to turn. And from inside the chapel you cannot even see the window properly: the view is blocked by the pipes of the organ – built for stirring masculine music, triumphalist and nineteenth-century in its confidence?

There is also confusion within – within each of us as we face our sexual dilemmas, as we try to speak of these things in courteously chosen words, as we try to focus the eye in a place of worship. Moreover, a company of religious people, more or less from the Christian tradition, find that they bring many styles and memories to their celebration of the Eucharist. It may be experienced by some (and it is certainly proclaimed as such) to be a focus of unity, the one place where we can all be together in the Sacrament of the Body and Blood of Christ. But it is also the place where pain and division are felt most acutely, and where confusion and anger rise to obscure and befuddle us. For myself, when bringing to worship the realities of sexuality, it is no use pretending that the Peace can be anything other than an earnest prayer that you and I and we may come to know the Peace of Christ and share it: I can receive it only with future tense in mind. And among fifty warm hugs there will always be a few people who at that moment pay the price of feeling excluded: their pain is too near the surface, and they cannot bear to touch.

These are sharp points that I am making – in more senses than one. At the very place of supposed security it seems that we can become exposed to the arrows of others within the household of faith. So, if there is confusion within, there is also hostility, and the confusion is compounded when the other is sensed as friend at one moment and as enemy the next. But we have to face the truth that even at the Eucharist we throw fiery darts at one another: some come from my unconscious and some from yours. And they hurt. And in these ecumenical days, I think they hurt more acutely. In the old days you could say the arrows came from 'them', Protestants or Catholics or whoever you perceived the wrongheaded opposition to be. The enemy without has become the enemy within, and we have not yet had the courage to be completely open with one another about our differences.

There are other dimensions to this hostility, to feelings of confusion. There are further religious ones: what of Jewish and agnostic participants in the conference? Then there is the fact that the main speakers and leaders of worship at this gathering concerned with matters of sexuality and spirituality have been men: they have dominated at least the public sessions.

Let me make the point sharper still. We have sung in the chapel that ever popular rouser of a hymn beloved of enthusiastic rallies, *And can it be that I shall gain?* I enjoy the tune, and I can sing it with some gusto. Even if I have had no blinding moment of conversion, I have known a few occasions on which I've blinked. And the words of the hymn do convey a profound truth about the grace of God. But if at the time of singing it I am aware of my own and others' sexuality, my voice dries up. Enthusiastic religion has too often spilled over into a denial of the sexual in general, and of the feminine and of sexual minorities in particular. As others around me sing cheerfully and vigorously, I begin to sense fiery darts coming from their unconscious. Now this may be unfair, and I am doubtless doing some projecting, but I think there is more to it than that. When I hear and see enthusiasm en masse, I see the smiles, but I also hear the daggers being unsheathed – and just because I am paranoid does not mean that they are not out to get me. I become cold and deeply afraid at what could emerge from the unconscious, especially the collective unconscious of a crowd at *any* kind of rally. Religious ones can be the worst. Dare I say that I feel uncomfortable at the parallels between evangelical rallies, papal masses, and fascist crowds? I feel compelled to ask, What are they ignoring? Are they demonstrating an idealism which by turns is sentimentally pious and one-sided and then condemning and cruel? What are they refusing to look at in themselves? It is so easy to become punishing on God's behalf: "Of course I love you, but it's for your own good . . ."

Are we sufficiently aware of this dynamic in ourselves? All of us are at times caught up in it, and we can reveal it suddenly at moments of emotional stress. So when I am aware of it in the atmosphere, I cannot sing. I have to put around me a protective shield because I do not know whence may come the darts. Members of the Church of Christ are not immune either way. Betrayals are always going on. Judas lives in each and all of us, even in our own familiar friends.

The hostility lies deep. We have inherited a knife, each of us, down the generations: we are all children of Cain. You have a knife; I have a knife; I know I could kill; my religious inheritance tells me it can be right to kill. I know I have the capacity to hurt; I know that I do hurt; I know that I have done so at this conference. And my religious inheritance tells me it can be right to exclude and to punish.

This applies both ways, but I do not know in advance that I can trust you, however good your intentions and however sincere and even truthful your words. Nor do you know that about me. I do not know where your knife is. You have been deeply hurt, your hand is unconsciously (at least sometimes) on the hilt of your dagger, ready to unsheathe it and stab in revenge.

Only insofar as we can work through our hostilities about sexuality, only insofar as we can own our own projections and recognize that we are so often twisting and turning the dagger into ourselves, only so will trust begin to flower and genuine love come alive.

Show me that you are at least aware that you have a knife. Show me that it is sheathed and your hand well away from it. If you can dare to be vulnerable and unbuckle the belt from which the dagger hangs, and lay it on one side, then I may be able to do the same. Then tears of penitence and reconciliation will begin to be a genuine possibility. But to do that both of us have to be open to profound change, change that comes in the depths of confession and absolution. Then, and only then, dare we exchange a gesture of true peace. Until the poverty-stricken and hard-pressed part of me can meet the poverty-stricken and hard-pressed part of you, we can but pray for each other's repentance, the repentance that is the willingness to change the heart's direction. And if you come at me in a crusading spirit, I have no choice but to defend myself, put up my shield, and try to bind your power.

These things take time, much more time than the four days or so of a conference. Yes, with two or three people, in one to one encounters, great gifts have been exchanged. Your vulnerability has been open to me and mine to you. Not that the whole story was told – nobody landed that big a fish! But there has been some healing, and that is the best reward of all the labour. And perhaps I used my beautiful old dagger as a not too painful scalpel. The wounded surgeon tries to heed Eliot and ply the steel so as to question only the distempered part.

In a workshop of a couple of dozen people, there was inevitably less trust, more pain and anger. But at least some of that emerged honestly, and I think it was contained by the grieving and hope that was also surfacing in the members of the group.

In the conference as a whole, in plenary sessions, those levels of exchange are impossible. We are bound to end in some frustration and with many questions. In an audience of this size I can dare to drop but hints of the vulnerabilities of my story. Yes, we yearn towards one another, but the reality is a great distance still between our finger tips.

Somehow we have to live with that sense of constriction. It is a narrow gate, bearable only in Christ. As individuals and as a company we travel through our wilderness, where there is no pleasure, no passion, no healing: maybe some will go away from this conference aware only of the winepress of the Wrath, which is Love's terrible face.

At such times there is only one place to go. As I stand with my shield up, I endeavour to place myself, in the words of an old hymn, 'hidden in thy wounded side'. I can trust only the Wounded One. That is the only ultimately safe place, not least if you have never been at home with your sexuality, perhaps never even aware of it, or if you have been wounded very early and have always found that sexuality to be a source of pain, even a life sentence, or if you have felt my words as stabs that have merely rasped your wound. You can then trust only the One who drank the Cup of pain and contradiction to the full, who said Yes to it all, and bore it all. Then the dramatic picture of the Lifeblood of Christ may still work its ancient power, his side slashed open by the knife, the Spear of the soldier, the Blood draining into the Cup, the Holy Grail of Myth and Truth. In that place, we may begin to be aware, alive, even in the midst of our constrictions, finding the narrow gate a life-giving place, however exhausting, and however sharp the point of intersection. The sword does indeed pierce all our hearts.

In the legend of the Holy Grail, as re-told by Wagner, the Guardian of the Grail, the Fisher-King, has been wounded in the groin. His healing can come only from the tip of the Spear of Christ which has been stolen. The knight Perceval, Parsifal, recaptures it, returning to touch the wound of the King, touch it with the still point, spear now used as scalpel, and the touch is accurate and the healing complete.

That story is echoed in the custom in the Greek Orthodox Church of using a small lance both to pierce the bread of communion and to cut it.

Living the pain within the Lifeblood, we are healed. We flow once more into a wide open space of joy and freedom, emerging as it were into an immense ocean under a starlit sky, inhabiting a great solitude where we are not lonely, but where there is room enough to contain all whom we love in our expanded hearts. As with Christ, the marks of the wounds do not disappear, but shine with glory. Into the wounds, into the space, there is now warmth and welcome for those who come. The empty womb of restored virginity (an innocence richer and deeper now, not inexperience, but having been through it all, a love that cannot possibly harm) is perpetually open, and others will find there a space where they can be free to breathe awhile and find some measure of healing.

Even if you have been wounded for life in the groin, you may still experience Perceval's touch – though even that may be a false hope in this world's terms. Maybe the most you will be given is the courage to bear the pain, in prayer and love for others. Yet the hope is that the Christ will still come to the tombs of deep darkness, where they say folk have been sleeping for generations, and cry in the deepest of dungeons, Awake from the dead.

I have been given permission to add this story as a coda, and I am indeed grateful to a latter-day 'Perceval' for this tale of a modern-day 'Fisher-King'.

He was much loved and respected, of his generation and not ours. Maybe he was one of the last to shut firmly the trap door leading to the cellar of his sexual desires. By the lights of the people of his day, which was the day before yesterday, he was an extraordinary spiritual guide, much of whose ministry was by letter, eleven hundred of which were waiting for him one year when he returned from a month's holiday. With hindsight, does this not seem like a promiscuity of people and of work?

He suffered heart trouble from early middle age, but disguised it as best he might. When he retired, he plummeted into deep depression. Flesh-body had to have its day, and its darker side proved all the stronger for having been denied. Did he allow too much the fantasy of others that puts their heroes of light on to pedestals? Yet he endured this overwhelming darkness. The suffering probably seemed more meaningless to him than it would do to us, but that is no judgment, only a spur to greater compassion among us. So much is out of balance, and we have been led, encouraged, blindly maybe, to deny and refuse the earth, the flesh, the feminine.

As a priest he respected the professionalism of doctors, and they his. He obeyed their orders unquestioningly, apart from a refusal to ease up on work. Again with hindsight, were not both trapped in dualism – the doctor looks after the body, the priest looks after the soul?

As he lay dying, he seemed fretful and anxious, his hands pushing down towards his legs as if to shake off the husk that flesh-body had become. A close friend keeping vigil that night put his hand on the dying man's thigh. It may have been the first time that he had ever been touched in that intimate place with care. And he relaxed, curled up peacefully as a child, and died a few hours later.

Was there some acceptance of flesh-body at the last? His wounded and often lonely self had loved within his lights and from the pain of his darkness, and the ways of contradiction had borne fruit in his ministry: a soul-body was ready to burst into flower. Perhaps a single touch was all that was needed to reconcile flesh-body being left behind with soul-body almost ready to go. The right touch at the right moment was enough. Perceval had healed the Fisher-King: he could die in peace.

APPENDICES

Appendix A
Past into present:
the Christian inheritance

I. JESUS, HUMAN SEXUAL

No one can *become* a human being out of the blue. To be genuinely human a person must emerge from the ongoing processes of life. This modern understanding is much like the ancient Hebrew: the fact that we are 'flesh' points to our being indissolubly bound up with all the life of earth.

Now Jesus shared the *same lump* of clay as we do. Otherwise he could not have been *a man*. The New Testament witnesses to the initiative of God in his birth – God is doing a new thing. But this newness is not the newness of novelty (*neos* in Greek), but that of the renewal of the old (*kainos* in Greek). The Spirit hovers and broods, and fashions, not a new plant, but a new blossoming, fulfilling a purpose that grows out of the past.

This makes us ask questions about the tradition of the virginal conception of Jesus. Certainly the 'Virgin Birth' has symbolic power: this man Jesus is believed to be uniquely of God, and his birth is God's initiative and through it God purposes a new thing. 'Virginity' is openness to life, to love, to God, perpetually. But are these truths necessarily bound up with a view of Jesus' birth that it by-passed sexual intercourse?

Jesus is reported to have had brothers and sisters. In Matthew 1.25 it is said that Mary and Joseph had no intercourse *until* her son had been born. Whatever truth there may be in Mary's perpetual 'virginity', it does not seem to be that she never had sexual intercourse. Thomas Aquinas, however, claimed that it was unthinkable that the virginal shrine should be so desecrated. Desecrated? What does that say about attitudes to sex? May it be that later feelings were projected back into the past and so dictated a view of how things must have been with the conception of Jesus? (This is a danger of

75

which the writer must be aware, including this one and these speculations.)

Sex is not the transmitter of original sin and therefore of itself 'tainted'. We are not sinful because of biological methods of reproduction. The potential for distortion is part of us simply because we have always breathed a distorted moral atmosphere. That is our collective inheritance, and we sin when we refuse the responsibility of becoming human, for that is the will of God for us. We sin insofar as and when we become aware of that calling and look and act the other way. In this sense Jesus did not sin, but the means of his birth and the processes of reproduction have nothing to do with it.

Various ancient Jewish sources claim a father for Jesus, and there is a trace of this tradition in John 8.41, where Jesus' critics try to score a point by saying, "We are not base born." Now if Jesus had been so born, we might have an instance of a fact so disturbing and radical that the Church was at best embarrassed and could refer to the truth only in code. Dare we suggest that God's purpose for Jesus was that he should be identified with the outcast by being born out of wedlock and known and regarded as such?

The genealogy in Matthew shows us that it is no barrier to belief that God's Spirit was at work in the birth of Jesus if Joseph was not the father. There are a number of irregularities in the ancestry. And even though the line is traced through the male, Matthew is at pains to include, somewhat unnecessarily, four women, all of whom had a dubious sexual reputation – Tamar, Rahab, Ruth, and Bathsheba. We need to remember too that God did not obey patriarchal rules, even in Old Testament time: he had a habit of choosing younger sons for his purposes, by-passing the elder.

Further, 'angel' is code for messenger, whether human or of some other order of being. It is interesting that the earliest Gospel, that of Mark, reports a young man at the tomb of Jesus when the women arrived, whereas Luke reports *two* men, and Matthew *an angel*. What kind of fact is being reported? Certainly the word 'angel' connotes the vibrant presence of God. Angels appear in the Gospels at particularly significant moments to alert us to the conviction that at these times God has drawn especially close. But angels were not always thought to be other than human. They could be entertained unawares. Pope Gregory knew that when he said of the slave boys in Rome, 'Not Angles, but Angels.' Does that suggest a reduction of the Archangel Gabriel to a handsome young stranger? Maybe, but either would have been an exciting figure, a bringer of life-giving energy, of the disturbing presence and power of God. And if Mary did indeed entertain an angel unawares, would this make her less worthy than the pure virgin of tradition, who had somehow been soiled by sex? Well, I do not want to dismiss angels out of hand. I would be loathe to lose my guardian angel, my sense of a supporting presence encouraging and warning me – or is that code for those hunches that press upon me from within from time to time? All I would claim is that the story of the Annunciation is not straightforwardly supernatural, not as clear-cut as we might have thought.

What then of Joseph? He did not penalize Mary according to the Law. He too became convinced, through dreaming (that other ambiguous method that God chooses in order to convey messages to us), that this child was specially of God. His acceptance is as much a marvel as Mary's. Yet that acceptance by either of them may not have been easy nor instantaneously complete. They may have struggled for some years to be serenely at home in their obedience. Accounts in retrospect often telescope the time-scale.

During those early months, perhaps Jesus did not have that perfect mothering and fathering that we assume he did. Was his conceiving and birthing altogether without pain and loss and troubling? Could he indeed have been human in any recognizable sense without that experience of bewilderment that is our common lot? What he did with it all as he grew up, aware of the presence and love of God, 'about his Father's business', is another matter altogether.

Behold the Man! Yes, but maybe with a troubled parenting, an uneasy time in the womb, born illegitimate and uncertain about his father, his own sexuality confused as a result. With that raw material, did he journey within during those early hidden years, steadily keeping his eye on all that troubled him and on God at the same time, in contemplation? Did he then reach the conviction that a total loving was possible out of the enduring of wounds that could not be healed in human terms, in the depths of solitude bearing them in God for others, so profoundly and accurately that people began to recognize in and through him nothing less than the full character and will and presence of God? Talk about entertaining angels unawares! His contemporaries who gave him meals were entertaining God unawares. Did Zaccheus wake up to that one as he mused in later years on his unusual and life-changing supper guest? Jesus was the one decisively and definitively at home in God, and the Divine Love shone through the pain, warming even the troubled flesh-body so that his touch was accurate and affirming and healing, giving delight and pleasure, while leaving others with an infinity of space in which to grow to be themselves. Thus he was the means of grace and the hope of glory.

His own human emotions come through particularly strongly in the stories of the rich young ruler, the centurion and his slave boy, Lazarus, Mary Magdalene, and the Beloved Disciple. He loved them all. Now it would be ludicrous to insist that any of those relationships must have been sexually focussed, but it would be equally ludicrous to suppose that Jesus' sexuality had nothing to do with them at all. Surely that sexuality was alive and its energy tapped. And if those relationships were not sexually focussed, that is not because they would have then be less than perfectly loving, but that it would not have been appropriate to enter the degree of human commitment implied, and would not have been an act of liberation for the other. Yet I can still find myself asking, Why not?

We all make Jesus in our own image, pursuing our own ideas of what we think perfect love would be like. And it is foolish to make anything much of an argument from silence. Nevertheless, it is useful for *us* to raise these questions about Jesus' birth and sexuality. It is salutary for us to ask ourselves why we react as we do. We are apt to forget how scandalous was (and is) the notion of the humanity of God, and how offensive to the people of his day was the manner of his death.

I have derived these speculations from John A. T. Robinson's book, *The Human Face of God*, and his scholarship is more secure than mine. He was not claiming any complete answers, but he was at pains to show how easily we seem to dehumanize Jesus, how much popular devotion tries to make him out to be a temporary divine visitor masked in human flesh but not really a human being. Robinson was concerned to be orthodox, and to re-assert that Jesus was indeed fully human, a first-century man, however difficult it might be for us to penetrate the centuries of distortion.

Hugh Montefiore gave this kind of sober speculation a further twist when he explored the possibility that Jesus' sexual orientation was towards his own sex. His argument was that there was no Jewish tradition of celibacy, that there are no records of Jesus' being married, and that an unusual and uncomfortable sexual orientation would have further identified him with the poor and hard-pressed. Again, there is no proof: the more interesting question is what effect this thinking has on *us*. Why could Jesus have not been so orientated? Could he not have loved with the love of God just as responsibly and accurately and creatively?

At least we can say this and be unquestionably orthodox: the Word was made flesh, God became a human being. This was God's pleasure and delight. So how do you respond to these statements? Where do you squirm and why? Jesus laughed ... (mmm, yes); cried ... (yes); sweated ... (well, yes, and it does say he even sweated blood in Gethsemane); ate oily foods . . . (never thought about his diet before); sneezed . . . (well, the roads could be dusty); and I hesitate to be specific about functions below the belt. I have emotional and cultural resistances which make it tough to keep asking certain questions and to be prepared for the answers. But to mention these things – is it in principle blasphemous, that is, taking God's name in vain, denigrating God? If so, why?

Jesus' sexuality was surely alive, however painful it may have been, however restrained in appropriate loving, but also a means of delight and pleasure shared, of creativity and union: to live such a life ourselves is surely to be not far from the Commonwealth of God.

II. BLESSINGS OF COVENANTS OF FRIENDSHIP

BLESSING – Covenant – Friendship: these are three strong biblical words which survive in Christian usage and which have profound meaning. They may be sufficient to indicate the shape and structure that will best enable the energies of sexuality serve the ends of true love and lasting joy. They are at the heart of the 'institution' of marriage but are not dependent on it.

Friendship ('philia') speaks of mutuality, affection, tenderness. A *covenant*, that which binds, is a container for the power of 'eros', the power which seeks a creative union, but which can be so passionate as to be blind and destructive. *Blessing* speaks of 'agape', the quality of loving that is other-regarding goodwill whatever the cost, and opens the personality to transfiguration. Here, then, is a way of humanizing and divinizing sexual desire, 'libido', a way of becoming persons-in-communion, on the way to the transforming of flesh-body into soul-body, of becoming selves-as-lovers. The union at its best is intimate and faithful, unlimited in time, enriching life by its creativity, and, however partially, embodying the love of God.

The way is not easy. Alan Ecclestone refers us to Mark Rutherford's novel, *Catherine Furze*, in which a non-church going doctor speaks of the attitude of the parish priest to his wife, who seems to the doctor to be ignoring the one person who is his alone to value. The man is guilty of desertion if he neglects his appointed place. Because another is not perfect, it is all too easy to give up the task of nourishing the good and enduring and forgiving the bad.

Reflecting on words that might express such a covenant shows that the way is tough:

"Of my own free will I have chosen to share my life with you, N, (and to care for such children as may be entrusted to us). In the presence of God and of these our witnesses, I affirm, renew, and deepen my promise to love you for ever, to do everything in my power for your well-being, to honour you as a temple of the living God, and to be loyal to you and full of faith in you, our life-day long."

Here we have a personal binding relationship of love sealed by self-giving to death and beyond, characterized by utter loyalty and a sense of deep belonging. As someone said, "We live in the same world – even if we often have great disagreements." A formal and public moment of covenanting can be a way of both cherishing and enlarging the friendship. The ways in which the relationship is expressed in flesh-body form will be a matter for responsible decision by the two people concerned. But a covenant of this kind can take the relationship beyond sexual attraction, legal contract, responsibility for children, and sharing a home. It may for some be exactly the equivalent of a monogamous marriage, but it could represent a binding just as deep between those who do not formally marry or who are committed in a same-sex relationship. A covenant may include making love sexually, drawing up legal contracts (including wills), conceiving or adopting children, and buying a home. But it need not depend on any of these things, and can also grow beyond them. We may also dare to see in this kind of commitment the best reflection of the relationship between human beings and God. That has often been portrayed in terms of a covenant and in terms of friendship. Abraham came to be known as a friend of God, and it was to such friendship that Jesus called his disciples, in the new covenant in his Blood.

Leonard Hodgson, in his book *Sex and Christian Freedom* (SCM Press, 1967, p. 106), says this of friendship: "Whether we are dealing with relations between men and women, or between persons of the same sex, there is a special enrichment of friendship which has its roots in their bodily sexual attraction for each other. They may be quite unaware of where it comes from. All that a man or a woman may know is that to be with some people gives them a kind of enjoyment that they do not have with others . . . "

Two people then, drawn to each other by a variety of attractions, into a special friendship, a friendship which comes to be best understood in terms of a covenant between them, and which is experienced as a mutual blessing. What does this word 'blessing' imply?

That God blesses us is to say that God accepts us, affirms us, encourages us, is generous towards us. Those who seek God's blessing on their friendship are saying, "We believe that God wants us to be together, that God delights in us, wills us to make love, and so be 'images', pictures as it were, of the abundant divine love which overflows in generosity to others."

This realization provokes a profound gratitude, and we in turn want to 'bless God', after the manner of Jewish prayers which begin, "Blessed are you, Lord . . ." To say this is to thank God for the presence and activity of divine love in our lives.

When we bless a thing, such as a ring, or a person or couple, we imply our belief that we can be channels of God's blessing to one another. This is focussed symbolically in the blessing given by a minister or priest, the one who represents the community, the Church, which as a body of people receives God's varied gifts. One of these is surely the special love that two people have for each other.

None of this is to underestimate the cost of such a friendship. That cost is vividly demonstrated in the story of the meeting of the Risen Christ with Peter. Peter, who had denied Jesus three times, was asked three questions to test his awareness of, and the depth of his commitment to, the kind of sacrifice required of him. Jesus asks, using the word 'agape', "Do you love me more than these?" Peter replies, using the word 'philia', "You know that I am your friend." Jesus says, within the bounds of what has been shown by that response to be possible, "Feed by lambs." Again Jesus asks Peter the same question, using the same words, and again Peter replies, "You know that I am your friend." The commission increased in scope: "Tend my sheep." Then Jesus asks a third question, this time using the word Peter has used in his replies, "Are you my friend?" In other words, "Are you really even my friend? Can you claim that much?" Peter remains steady at last (almost the Rock?), without suggesting that he could do more than he knew he was capable of: "You know everything; you know that I am your friend." The firebrand has become a sober realist, and knows the next step he can take. "Feed my sheep," says Jesus.

So failure, forgiveness, honesty, realism, new starts, are all possible, even within the closest and most demanding of relationships. And was even the binding of Jesus and Peter, here described with a great delicacy of touch, and now set to flower through the distance and separation that is always needed if the depths of love are to be sounded, rooted in a mutual attraction of each to other that tapped the energies of their human sexuality?

III. THE SACRAMENTAL

A SACRAMENTAL understanding of sexuality perceives it as more than incidental or physical. It recognizes that the sexual *participates* in the spiritual, is an intrinsic element in any impulse of embodied human beings towards God. Most people seem to treat sexuality as mere sign, ie. in the end it is not necessary, and on the way it may be utterly misleading. But a sacramental approach insists that anything material can participate in the divine, and can often communicate what cannot be expressed adequately in words. So it is with water and bread and wine and sex. Communion is interpenetration, coinherence with the greater Love that is known from the within of our flesh-body meetings as well as not being contained by them. The prayer that we may dwell in Christ and Christ in us includes the dimension of the sexual. We are in process of becoming body-words of God.

Moreover, we do not experience these things solely as individuals. In fact the sacramental vision is of true community and of earth transformed. The individual may be climbing Jacob's Ladder. Together we are invited to dance Sarah's Circle.

Of course it is not always like this, but there is something disappointing about sex without mystery, just as there is something disappointing about eucharist without mystery – too many bare words and not enough body in it, not enough bread. Flowers, icons and photographs, incense and scent, candles, music, and singing and poetry – these are all part of the sensuousness of love-making and eucharist-making. Yes, we may need manuals on sexual technique and we may need the labours of liturgical scholars on ancient texts, but heaven preserve us from sex and worship using their respective insights alone!

I think the details of the sequence of love-making and eucharist-making are illuminated when seen in parallel. There is the mutual greeting at the beginning. There is a prayer that we may be willing to be open and truthful to the Other who is Lover, for otherwise love cannot be made, it won't happen, it won't work out, it won't come right. We do not have to make an effort to *do* anything: we have simply to be open. The fact that it is simple does not, however, make it easy, and most of us fall at this first hurdle. (Well, it is more like tripping over our own feet, since there is nothing out there to stumble over.)

Next comes the conversation, the dialogue, the ministry of the Word, of words. Through language we get to know one another better, we learn more of God. This is followed by the affirmation of each other in trust and belief – the Creed, a renewal of promises made in covenant. Then there is the acknowledgment that what we are doing is 'bigger than both of us'. In fact it is intrinsic to the love of the whole world. It is intercession, it is the gathering up of others in mind's eye and heart's ease into our love-making.

Because of what has been said so far, confession and absolution may well be needed, followed by the deliberate and sensitive touch of healing and peace.

'Offertory' speaks of laying oneself down, a naked offering, a gift of oneself to the act and to the other. 'Thanksgiving' speaks of rejoicing and of pleasure, of a recital of all the past gifts, of enjoyment, and of awe in the presence of the Holy. 'Fraction' speaks of a loss of control and a breaking of the boundaries. 'Communion' speaks of a mutual giving and receiving of new life.

Following a time of silence and of simply resting in each other's embrace, we are impelled by the encounter to love more widely all that has been celebrated, to love the other, and the Other, and the others and the whole earth: the creativity of Making Love and Making Eucharist flows out to embrace the world.

This sacramental view of food and sex and worship as means of grace can be put broadly in diagrammatic form, in the right-hand column in what follows, with the realities of a non-sacramental understanding in the left-hand column.

IMPERSONAL – dia-bolic: split apart	PERSONAL – sym-bolic: joined together
SEX	
Central nervous system	Autonomic nervous system
Genital sensation & fantasy	Bodily, wave-like sensation & no fantasy
Pelvic rigidity	Pelvic movement
Rigid – jerk	Spontaneous – flow
Compulsive, mechanical, libido on the loose	Passionate and erotic
	Affectionate and tender
	Willing the other's good
Hatred of the flesh	Delight in the flesh
Mechanical thrust	Rhythmic swive
Possessive insecurity	Liberating trust
Relief of loneliness	Acceptance of space between
FOOD	
Reconstituted cream cake	Freshly extracted apple juice
Eat to exist	Candlelit meal for two
Grab, stuff	Knowing what is enough
Obesity and anorexia	Feasting and fasting
WORSHIP	
Sentimental or harsh voice	Bodily present humane voice
Opium	Communion
Encourages fanaticism	Encourages friendship
Indulges fantasy & illusion	Embraces the truth of crucifixion and resurrection

IV. SEXUALITY AND DISCIPLESHIP

THROUGH a positive appreciation and experience of our sexuality we begin to sense meaning and direction for our lives. By means of it we reach out to others to touch them, in healing and in pleasure. By means of it we know what it is to be at one with another and to create with and through another. We may even know ecstasy and see stars.

So the disciples found their lives enhanced when touched by Jesus who called them. Words had new authority, touch conveyed healing. Through words and touch, truth was shared – and pleasure? Was a new kind of loving being created through their relationship one with another and with Jesus?

But our sexuality is also the occasion of the negative in our experience. We know wounding and disintegration, betrayal, possessiveness, jealousy, loss. Meaning dissolves into meaninglessness, joy disintegrates into sadness, fiery flames collapse to dust and ashes. We feel enormously let down.

Jesus steadfastly went to Jerusalem to face all that is negative in human life. The disciples were bewildered and afraid. They began to scatter, they abandoned Jesus, they betrayed and denied him. The demands of love were too great. For something more was at stake than fulfilment in this world's terms of pleasure, popularity, and even healing. Because they could not see what it was, despite hints of transfiguration, they fell apart.

So we too know emptiness, monotonous and monstrous space, the pain of loneliness, insecurity, forsakeness. And we endure through a dark night of waiting for a new dawn that is not of our making. Indeed we cannot expect to see it until our eyes have got used to the dark. At best there is a slim hope within us of a new resolution, a new dimension that will give us an appreciation of an unknown whole that is greater than the sum of the parts that, until now, we have known.

For the disciples, something better was in store beyond the

loss, beyond crucifixion: an all-pervasive, transforming presence, God as Holy Spirit revealed in a new way, in whose Presence they saw Jesus anew, risen from the dead, and in whose Presence they lived and spread the Gospel.

Everything is of sexuality and everything is of spirituality, and both are of God in this new age: it is characterized by a total spiritual-spirited-embodied loving. The raw yearning desire, so easily out of hand, is the material out of which God as Spirit is fashioning a new glory. The earthy body of flesh and blood will be made like Christ's glorious body, and for that day the whole creation yearns with eager longing. And God shall be all in all.

[With due acknowledgment to Alan Jones, in whose book *Soul-Making* this understanding of the disciples' pilgrimage is explored.]

Appendix B
Some resources for worship

I. A HYMN

WORD made Flesh! We see Christ Jesus
    Sharing our humanity,
Loving, graceful, always truthful,
    Close to others bodily,
Full of passion, full of healing,
    Touch of God to set them free.

Wonderful are these our bodies,
    Flesh and blood to touch and see,
Place of pain and contradiction,
    Yet of joy and ecstasy,
Place of passion, place of healing,
    Touched by God who sets us free.

O how glorious and resplendent,
    Fragile body you shall be,
When endued with so much beauty,
    Full of life and strong and free,
Full of vigour, full of pleasure,
    That shall last eternally.

Glory give to God the Lover,
    Grateful hearts to the Beloved,
Blessed be the Love between them,
    Overflowing to our good;
Praise and worship, praise and worship,
    To the God whose Name is Love.

The third verse is late 15th century, tr. J. M. Neale,
and found as part of the hymn, 'Light's abode,
celestial Salem', *New English Hymnal*, 401, to the tune
Regent Square.

II. A PRAYER

DEAR GOD, Giver of life, Bearer of pain, Maker of love,
   affirming in your incarnation the goodness of the flesh,
may the yearnings of our bodies be fulfilled
   in sacraments of love,
and our earthly embracings be enjoyed
   as a foretaste of the glory to come,
in the light of the Resurrection of Jesus Christ,
   our Companion, our Lover, and our Guide.

III. A VERSION OF PART OF
1 CORINTHIANS 13

I MAY have the gift of many languages and of great eloquence, but if I have no love in my heart, I am but a hollow gong or a clanging cymbal. I may be a man of God and understand and explain every hidden truth, but if I have no love, I am nothing. I may have faith enough to move mountains, I may give away all that I have to feed the hungry, I may even seek the glory of a martyr, but if I have no love, I achieve precisely nothing.

Love is patient and kind. Love knows no envy. Love never clings, is never boastful, conceited, or rude. Love is never selfish, never insists on its own way. Love is not quick to take offence. Love keeps no score of wrongs, nor gloats over the sins of others. Love rejoices in the truth. Love is tough: there is nothing it cannot face. Love never loses trust in human beings or in God. Love never loses hope, never loses heart. Love still stands when all else is fallen . . .

Now we see only puzzling reflections in a mirror; but then we shall see face to face. Now I know little of the truth; then my knowledge will be whole, like God's knowledge of me. In a word, but three things last for ever – faith, hope, and love: and it is love that crowns them all.

IV. SOME QUESTIONS FOR A COVENANT

N and N, you are about to make a solemn promise. Do you believe God has called you to live together in love? *We do.*

Do you promise to be loyal to each other, never allowing any other relationship to come before the one you are about to affirm? *We do.*

Will you give yourselves to each other wholeheartedly and without reserve? *We will.*

Will you, under God, recognize each other's freedom to grow as individuals and allow each other time and space to do so? *We will.*

Will you do all in your power to make your life together a witness to the love of God in the world? *We will.*

N, will you give yourself wholeheartedly to N, sharing your love and your life, your joys and sorrows, your health and sickness, your riches and poverty, your success and failure? *I will.*

Will you, the chosen witnesses this day of N and N, do all in your power to support and strengthen them in the days ahead? *We will.*

V. AN EXCHANGE OF PROMISES

OF my own free will I have chosen to share my life with you, N,
[and to care for such children as may be entrusted to us].
In the presence of God and of these our witnesses
I affirm, renew, and deepen my promise to love you for ever,
[to do everything in my power for your well-being,]
to honour you as a temple of the living God,
and to be loyal to you and full of faith in you,
our life-day long.

VI. *FROM* THE PROPHET *BY KAHLIL GIBRAN*

LET there be space in your unity. Love each other, but let it not
be bondage. Fill each other's cup to the full, but do not drink
from the same cup. Give bread to each other, but do not eat
from the same piece. Sing and dance together and be happy,
but be each of you alone, like the strings of the lute are by
themselves though trembling with the same melody. Give
your hearts to each other, but not just for preserving; because
only the hand of Life can keep your hearts. Stand together, but
do not stand too close; as the pillars of the temple stand each by
themselves, and the oak and the cypress cannot grow in each
other's shade.

VII. *A SONNET BY WILLIAM SHAKESPEARE*

LET me not to the marriage of true minds
Admit impediments. Love is not love
Which alters when it alteration finds,
Or bends with the remover to remove:
O no! it is an ever-fixèd mark
That looks on tempests and is never shaken;
It is the star to every wandering bark,
Whose worth's unknown, although his height is taken.
Love's not Time's fool, though rosy lips and cheeks
Within his bending sickle's compass come:
Love alters not with his brief hours and weeks,
But bears it out even to the edge of doom.
    If this be error and upon me proved,
    I never writ, nor no man ever loved.

VIII. FROM A LETTER OF BEDE JARRETT

You must not be afraid of looking for God in the eyes of a friend. He is there. You can at least be sure of that. To love others is not to lose Him but if possible to find Him in them. He is in them. You don't lose God by loving others; you will find Him if you love them. You will miss finding Him only if you merely love yourself in them. That is the blinding nature of passion; it is self-love masquerading under a very noble disguise . . . You must indeed be afraid of supplanting God's unique position by substituting one of his workmanship for it; but you will only overcome that danger one way. Other people would find other ways. Your way is a very simple but hard way. It is to go on loving Y; if you stop loving him you'll miss God. If you thought the only thing was to retire into your shell you'd never see how lovely God was. You must love Y and look for God in Y.

Appendix C
Meditations on power

Words of the powerful in the land –
    haranguing, harassing, beating down,
    sly and clever, leaving the hearers dumb –
    words no longer heartfelt,
    their birth in the wordsmith's forge long forgotten,
    cruel now, and hard.
The poor, deprived of their language,
    rich oral language of their place,
    robbed of words that have meaning,
    stolen by peddlers of distortions and lies:
    the oppressed turn into themselves and they howl –
    and the only way to relate is to hit.
A few, stung by the same hurting,
    search for words of new beauty,
    of clarity and truth.
They seek con-solation.
    that we may 'warmed in the sun together',
    words alive and shimmering between us,
    sensuous words, full of passion,
    words charged with sexual power,
    enfleshed by throat and tongue and lips,
    engodded words creating and making love.

❖

PRAY first for their *repentance* –
   those who kill animals for anything but food,
      especially those who relish the slaughter,
         and those who have exterminated whole species . . .
   sexually excited torturers in interrogation rooms
      and rapists on city streets . . .
   demanding forceful men who take their so-called pleasure
      and leave humiliated and exhausted women without a
      second thought . . .
   peddlers of pornography that exploits women
      and shows contempt and hatred . . .
   religious fanatics who hate the flesh
      and seek to punish those who are different from
      themselves . . .

And may the oppressed rise with anger and compassion,
   claiming their place under the sun,
   open to forgiving those who have shown a changed heart,
   giving voice to those who have no voice of their own . . .

And may the oppressor and the victim within each of us
   begin by turning face to face . . .

❖

IN REPENTANCE for thoughts, words, and deeds –
  hating the flesh
  loathing the feminine
  unleashing of lust
  coldly withdrawing
  raping the earth
  bruising a lover
  restlessly roaming
  short-lived excitement
  the flesh as machine
  refusing to be earthed
  sexual desire uncontained
  hiding behind walls of words
  burning with fanatical zeal
  unaffected by doubt
  humiliating another
  dominating another
  ignoring another
  scything whole peoples
  cold hating murder
  no connection with heart-warmth
  arrogantly solemn
  living the lie
  refusing to be playful
  no pleasure or laughter

❖

Appendix D
Meditations on loving in God

THE HUM of a generator
   bringing to vibrant life
   material stuff of earth!
How much energy can the human organism stand,
   can *this* organism stand that is my flesh-body self?
Ecstasy may be well-nigh intolerable pleasure,
   the vibrations so strong and overwhelming
   that pleasure becomes pain.
The hurt resonates in the very place where healing is deeply
   sought.
O this place of painful contradiction,
   of pleasurable celebration!
So very near to pleasure from deliberate hurting,
   or from deliberately being hurt . . .

It is a subtle energy,
   the heavenly in the guts of earth,
   the hellish most likely at the very gates of heaven,
   where angels entertain unawares –
   or are they devils in cloaks of light?
Or is it God indeed so very close
   with hovering and pulsing wings
   in the vibrations of passionate love?
Devilish if there be no laughter, no truth,
   but might we yet find God in human loins?

Is this the place where we must be most profoundly moved,
   where we can know the Love that moves the sun and moon
   and stars?

❖

FALL in love with God . . .
Why do you hesitate?
  Reserve?
  Thinking that being in love with God implies no human
    in-loving?
  Living with a picture of God as Controller?
After all, to be in love is to have lost control.
  And the projection of control on to God –
  that is a tough one to learn to withdraw.
But God is pure unbounded Love,
  God-is-for-you,
  God-is-for-your-well-being.
That is what God's nature is.
God desires you to flourish,
  God enjoys nurturing and giving,
  is in loving.
God is absolutely intimate,
  within, totally understanding.
God is absolutely beyond,
  other, totally challenging.
So nurture your capacity to become aware of this
  Mysterious Other Within.
Leisurely think about nothing,
  and open your heart and mind to this Impossible Beauty.
Open your heart-mind.
Fall in love with God.

❖

Do NOT cling to God.
You must separate yourself from the divine parent
  if you are to be truly human.
You are afraid to do this because you do not know
  if you can stand upright without support.

So you talk of a God who is greater than you,
  and there is truth in that.
And you talk of a God whose Love is inexhaustible
  and who lures and beckons to you out of the future,
  towards whom you yearn,
  and that also is true.
But there can be no true love
  without a respectful distance,
  one from the other.
It is true that the separation is experienced
  from the *within* of love.
  but because you resist *love*,
  you do not yet see it and know it from the inside,
  where there is both appropriate closeness
  and appropriate distancing.
You need the space between in which to grow
  and in which to choose and exercise your freedom.
God is not you:
  in you, yes;
  greater than you, yes;
  beyond you, yes;
  and also not you, other than you.
For your sake God hides away,
  and your taking leave of God
  is as much part of the life of faith
  as your coming home to God.
It is often easier to think of yourself close to God
  while remaining remote and distant from those around you.
But you cannot truly love God
  if you are not close to your neighbour.
You may need to be more distant from God
  in order to learn human loving –
  and to discover again that God is already there before you.

❖

You do not like your sexuality because you do not know God.
When Adam and Eve broke with the Companion,
  they were immediately ill at ease with themselves as bodies,
  they were ashamed.
And the shame bred lust
  (it was not the other way round).
Then, consumed by desires that were no longer recognized
  as the desire for God,
their (and our) sexuality went out of control –
  or became sternly controlled.
You may even explore the range of sexual possibility,
  even believe that sex is all there is,
and then end up profoundly dissatisfied.
Go back to the place of being ill at ease,
  of desire for the Companion,
  of putting sexuality in its place of mystery,
but now as a befriended mystery.
It goes wrong when unfriendly.
When you have befriended your sexuality,
  you will know from within the moments of its expression
  that will be appropriate and full of delight.

❖

BECAUSE human beings are made in the image of God
  and are destined to live in God's presence for ever,
and because Christ is God become human
  and we are his sisters and brothers,
then people are absolutely important.
Those who do not love their sisters and brothers
  are not loving, cannot love, God.
I love you because you are you,
  and because I love God who is in you.

I cannot love you as a by-product of my love for God –
    for I am loving God even as I love you.
I am committed to you whatever –
    even if you slay me.

❖

SAY YES to a love
    that will drag you through the depths,
    scour your emotions,
    scar and heal your heart,
    and lift you to the skies.

❖

THANK God the Gospel has a lot of pelvis in it.

❖

IN LIVING the youness of you,
    be prepared to go outside the gate in giving all.
But first, keep asking,
    What is my deepest desire now?
In desiring to give yourself utterly,
    do not do so prematurely,
    before you have become the fullest self
    that it is possible for you to become.
There are many lesser desirings and givings
    that must have their place.
Not least among these are affection, companionship,
    falling asleep in the arms of those who love you,
    the making of love.
And when such lesser desires are being fulfilled,
    rejoice in what is, however incomplete.
If you expect all,
    you will be worshipping an idol,
    not enjoying life with another human being.

❖

REJOICE if you discover and are discovered
    by the one who in human terms matters most to you
    and to whom you matter most.
But do not pine if this is not your path.
Cherish those who do matter to you very much indeed.

✠

You imagine that the difference between 'marriage' and
    'celibacy'
    is defined by the presence or absence of genital sexual
    loving.
But if you are 'married',
    you will find yourself saying,
      "Our relationship matters to me
      more than anything else in the world."
If you are 'celibate',
    (and you may actually have a marriage partner),
    you will find yourself saying,
      "Our relationship matters to me
      more than any other relationship,
      but something else matters more."
Now it is not God who is that something else.
    for that would be to put in opposition human and divine
    loving.
No, both these ways of human loving are paths
    which will involve hard choices and decisions,
    but will, when faithfully pursued,
    show forth the divine.
    'What matters more' is some creative endeavour,
    an art, a vocation, a quest,
    through which the divine is shown in a person's life
    more fully than could be the case any other way.

✠

IN THE WAYS of your bodily loving and relating,
      choose that which, in the given circumstances,
      will increase intimacy, love, creativity.
Do not ask, Will we have sex?
Rather, Will we share life with delight,
      will we be making love?
Do not seek, as of first importance, in time or desire,
      the immediately attractive.
Test the worth.
Learn to pause.
      and to bear the pain which rises in the pause.
But if you do say No to a particular course of action,
      let your assent flow with that No.
Say No only if you can say it gladly, wholeheartedly,
      only for the sake of a more profound Yes.
Let the seeking be for *God's* way.
Let there be no grabbing of what you desire,
      but do not refuse to draw close
      out of a fear of being devoured or overwhelmed.

❖

MAY you say of each person who is part of your life,
      however fleetingly,
      I need you in order to be myself.

❖

THE COMMONWEALTH of God is richly there,
   within you and around you.
The Divine Creator sows the seed,
   the potential creation in embryo,
   in the cells of your being,
   even the potential for the unexpectedly new.
You grow towards and discover the fulfilment
   by reaching out and striving –
   and also by deepening and letting be.
And a warm loving of others grows,
   spanning age and sex,
   a loving that is joyous and sexual and spiritual and whole.
Go then with the grain of who you are now,
   and be open to every possibility,
   which will not be an exchange of one thing for another,
   nor a substitution,
   but an adding,
   to a more abundant and mutual enrichment.

❖

You cannot be creative without knowing what it is to be lonely.
This is because what you create is unique.
Otherwise it would merely be a copy,
And you cannot be creative
   without always being dissatisfied and sometimes des-
   pairing.
Whatever you create may be good enough,
   may be adequate,
   may do,
   but it will never be perfect.
This means unhappiness,
   for the vision is always beyond your ability to give it shape,
   it is always going on ahead of you.

❖

PLEASURE for yourself (self-love)
   and giving pleasure to others (gift-love)
   are one and the same movement.
Self-gift is the intensest pleasure
   and in the pleasure it loses all sense of moralizing.
   'Flourishing' and 'making flourish' are one.
This goes against the grain of your inheritance, but –
   believe in the spontaneous goodness of yourself;
   let go the dutiful controller;
   recognize your desire for endless bliss.
God is not a patrolman but a friend and lover.
Only compulsive tyrants insist you do what they dictate.
But in desiring approval you gave of yourself
   and suppressed, even repressed, your self-love.
So the giving of yourself tends to be an enslavement,
   and this breeds not self-love but self-hatred.

❖

YOU do not need another to be your other half,
   as though you were bound to be incomplete if you live alone.
But you do need others
   that they may enable you to be that complete person
   which you already have it in you to become.

❖

BE gentle with your wounds.
Remember that wounds always leave their mark –
    even the emotional hurts are still trapped
    in the cells and muscles of your organism.
You can slide over them of course,
    even be physically sexual,
    and yet remain on the rigid surface,
    not allowing the wounds to be touched,
    and so getting by with short-lived excitement.
But you need to let the wounds be touched
    by a healing love,
and you won't be able to do this
    until you trust the healing lover enough
    to be assured that your opening up
    will not be to further pain.

❖

WHEN you are in the mood of desperate loneliness
    and compulsive habit,
you are indeed 'beside yourself'.
Come back gently 'to yourself',
    come 'to your senses'.
Be 'within yourself'.
Allow the 'masculine' and the 'feminine' to nourish each other
    and to make love within.
Be 'within your Self' –
    that perhaps is the more enGodded and emBodied way of
    putting it.

❖

INNOCENT love desires no harm.
Hence it is more trustworthy than passionate love.
  'Innocent' love need not mean 'without experience'.
  for it can be a mature and disinterested love
    on the far side of the passion that is both sexual and
      suffering.
Projections and idols and mirrors are not mixed in with it.
And you need to experience that love
  where you are most vulnerable – in the groin.
And that is precisely why a directly sexual and passionate love
  can never of itself complete the healing it seems to promise.
Only a sure and steady love can do that:
  the love that is without limits –
    nothing that the other can do is able to destroy it,
    however much the other may hurt;
  the love that does not control –
    the one who loves accepts that love is precarious
    and that tragedy may come,
    yet will always seek to redeem
    rather than take revenge;
  the love that is not detached –
    the one who loves accepts the fact
    that deep involvement with another
    means constant exposure
    and constant vulnerability.

❖

GUARD and protect your creativity,
   the divine flame,
   the infinite becoming finite in you,
   coming to birth in you.
Do this for each other.
This is one of the meanings of your love.
Such a love can focus on the beyond,
   on the future.
You will be able to say of anything you create,
   Part of N is in that.
N will be able to say of anything you create,
   Part of me is in that.
The cost is to be uniquely loyal to the Creative Source,
whilst recognizing that each needs the other
   to do something which the surface self will not like,
that is,
   to keep that loyalty primary and unswerving.

❖

Do not be afraid of being close,
   of loving each other,
   of taking risks,
   of weakness,
   of being vulnerable.
Let love cast out fear.
Let steady warmth melt anxiety.

❖

Let your love be exclusive, but not exclusive:
    special, but not excluding.
You do not matter to each other more than anything else
    or more than anyone else in the world.
But you matter to each other in a unique way
    that no one can replace,
and that matters to each of you very much indeed.

❖

You *say* that you want to claim him wholeheartedly *for you* –
    such is the total demand of inloveness.
But he cannot fill that aching void
    which you must bear in ever-deepening love *for him*.
No human being can fill ĭat void:
    even God doesn't.
Only living from the depth of the void
    can the life of God grow in you.
Inloveness can so often be a snare,
    an avoiding of truth,
    a making an idol of the other,
    an escape from real closeness,
    a false simplifier.
Inloveness makes all manner of irrational demands on the
    other and excuses for the other,
rather than the truth in love which says,
    I am disappointed,
    I am grieving,
    I am angry,
    I am afraid,
trusting that the deepest love
    can contain and transform all that is painful.

❖

LET there be space.
Remember that the ones you love in your heart
   are but guests in your soul.
Do not claim too much of his space,
   anything that is beyond the integrity of his giving.
He will be steadfast:
   you must withdraw your projections.
He will bear with your weaknesses:
   you must bear with the anxieties that have nothing to do
      with him.

❖

RECOGNIZE that much 'noise' from the past
   gets in the way of your truly loving.
And be grateful for his love,
   for its assurance can enable you,
   in the spaces and the distances,
   to dare to listen more closely to that 'noise',
   distinguishing sounds from clamour.
   love from inlove.

❖

BE thankful that the experience of being sexually vulnerable,
    in love and saying so,
has not taken away the conviction
    that you are still loved.
You *can* trust him,
    you *can* believe in his love for you.
Yes, you wobble with fear –
    and that may well be the fear of intimacy
    more than the fear of rejection you suppose it to be.
But live the fear –
    and live the grief and anger too.
Let them warm you out of the cold,
    and do not leave your feelings to become detached,
    and so harsh and bitter.
Of course you grieve and are angry,
    and you howl,
    Why can't you love me the way I want?
But the truth is that that kind of loving
    cannot be creative for you
    and is not part of his truth.
And he does love you in the way you *need*.
Blast him and bless him, yes.
That respects him and humbles you.
Do not burden him with the responsibility of being God –
    not *perfectly* loving –
    and even that does not often feel like love –
but be glad that he will bear the responsibility
    of being human with you.

❖

On the Causey Pike Ridge

ROMAN centurion far from vineyards,
Marching south from High Street to Ravenglass,
Do you, like me, delight in cold beauty,
Blue and white from February's sun on snow?
Or are you tortured by this breath of warmth,
Northern laughter mocking your yearning flesh,
Worse than winter winds in this your exile?

❖

Above Wastwater

THE WIND splits bone from bone
As two friends lean into the flank
Of Illgill Head.
Water is locked in ice,
And ice is clamped to rock,
Borrowdale Volcanic,
Its furnace long forgotten . . .

Only,
An echo of that original blaze
Is heard in spring's first murmuring:
Silver flecks dance free of clinging grey
Into moments of meeting
That weave together flesh and flesh.

❖

IF you dwell in the Divine Love,
   generous, self-giving,

if you respond to that Love
   with the whole of your being,

if you love your neighbour as yourself,

if you love others
   in the way pioneered by Jesus of Nazareth,
      utterly, with no defences and no limits,
      whatever the cost,
      loving even your enemy,

then, as surely as night follows day,

you will never use force –
   though you will refuse to let others escape from love and
   truth;

you will never use others merely to provide what you want –
   though you will respect and express your own needs;

you will never take advantage of others' ignorance or
   immaturity –
      though you will try to increase their knowledge and wisdom;

and you will find yourself loving others

    passionately, on wings of flame:

    fiercely, eager for truth;

    honestly, with no illusions;

    courageously, bearing the hurts of others;

    gently, with no hint of cruelty;

    sensitively, acknowledging the integrity of others,
        and giving them space;

    respectfully, without seizing others in a possessive spirit;

    responsibly, aware of the consequences of what you do;

    trustfully, overcoming your fear of rejection;

    welcomingly, accepting others as they are;

    always open to forgiving others,
        even when tempted to turn away,
        steadily waiting for the one who has hurt you to turn back;

    generously, without thought of return;

    wholeheartedly, full of faith and loyalty;

and you will find yourself also willing and glad

    to receive love,

    to be loved by others in equal measure.

❖

Some reading around the theme

MULLED OVER

Anon. *Reflections in a moving stream.* 1982 [unpublished]

Baldwin, James. *Another country.* Michael Joseph, 1963

Burton, Jack. *Transport of delight.* SCM, 1976

Eliot, T. S. 'Four quartets'. in *Collected poems.* Faber, 1963

Julian of Norwich. *Revelations of divine love.* Penguin, 1966

Moore, Sebastian. *The crucified is no stranger.* DLT, 1977

Rilke, R.M. *Letters to a young poet.* Norton, New York, 1934

Teilhard de Chardin, P. 'The evolution of chastity' in *Toward the future.* Collins, 1974

Vanstone, W.H. *Love's endeavour, love's expense.* DLT, 1977

READ

Bonhoeffer, D. *Letters and papers from prison.* SCM, 1967

Ecclestone, Alan. *Yes to God.* DLT, 1975

Eco, Umberto. *The name of the rose.* Secker & Warburg, 1983

Jones, Alan W. *Soul-making.* SCM, 1985

Lawrence, D.H. *Lady Chatterley's lover.* Penguin, 1960

Leech, Kenneth. *True God.* Sheldon, 1985

Levi, Primo. *If this be a man.* Abacus, 1987

Levi, Primo. *If not now when?* Michael Joseph, 1986

Montefiore, H.W. 'Jesus revelation of God' in ed. Pittenger, N. *Christ for us today.* SCM, 1967

Nelson, James. *Embodiment.* Augsburg, Minnesota, 1978

Nelson, James. *Between two gardens.* Pilgrim Press, New York, 1983

Robinson, J.A.T. *The Body.* SCM, 1957

Robinson, J.A.T. *The human face of God.* 1973

REFERRED TO

CALLAGHAN, Morley. *They shall inherit the earth.* Macgibbon &
Kee

DWORKIN, Angela. *Our blood.* Women's Press, 1982

MASCALL, E.L. *The Christian universe.* DLT, 1966

NICHOLS, J. *Men's liberation.* Penguin, New York, 1975

POHIER, J. *God in fragments.* SCM, 1985

SINGER, J. *Androgny.* RKP, 1977

WATTS, Alan. *Nature, man and woman.* Thames and Hudson,
1958

❖

I wish particularly to acknowledge a debt to the work of
Sebastian Moore and W. H. Vanstone for inspiration for the
meditations on pp. 98, 100(1), and 104(2), and on p. 107,
respectively.